CW00411105

Saving Our ⏤

Saving Our Streams

The Role of the Anglers' Conservation
Association in Protecting
English and Welsh Rivers

ROGER BATE

The Institute of Economic Affairs

First published in Great Britain in 2001 by
The Institute of Economic Affairs
2 Lord North Street
Westminster
London SW1P 3LB
in association with Profile Books Ltd

Copyright © The Institute of Economic Affairs 2001

The moral right of the author has been asserted.

All rights reserved. Without limiting the rights under copyright reserved above,
no part of this publication may be reproduced, stored or introduced into a
retrieval system, or transmitted, in any form or by any means (electronic,
mechanical, photocopying, recording or otherwise), without the prior written
permission of both the copyright owner and the publisher of this book.

A CIP catalogue record for this book is available from the British Library.

ISBN 0 255 36494 6

Many IEA publications are translated into languages other than English or are
reprinted. Permission to translate or to reprint should be sought from the
General Director at the address above.

Typeset in Stone by MacGuru
info@macguru.org.uk

Printed and bound in Great Britain by Hobbs the Printers

CONTENTS

TABLES AND FIGURES

THE AUTHOR

Roger Bate founded the Environment Unit at the Institute of Economic Affairs in 1993 and co-founded the European Science and Environment Forum in 1994. He undertook a research project on water allocation in South Africa for the South African Water Research Commission. This research formed part of his PhD at Cambridge University.

Dr Bate is the editor of *What Risk?* (Butterworth Heinemann, 1997), a collection of papers that critically assess the way risk is regulated in society. He has also written several scholarly papers and numerous shorter scientific articles for newspapers and magazines, including the *Wall Street Journal, The Financial Times, Accountancy* and *LM*. His most recent book is *Life's Adventure: Virtual Risk in a Real World* (Butterworth Heinemann, 2000).

The author can be contacted on rbate@iea.org.uk

ACKNOWLEDGEMENTS

Many people have helped me over the years with my interest in the Anglers' Conservation Association (ACA). Fred Smith of the Competitive Enterprise Institute in Washington, DC, first proposed the idea of a study; Allen Edwards and Jane James from the ACA, and Peter Carty and Simon Jackson, the ACA's solicitors, helped with information; Terry Anderson and those at the Political Economy Research Center (PERC) in Montana, especially Clay Landry, provided me with the conditions conducive to writing. Matt Ridley, Roger Meiners, Don Leal, Dan Benjamin, Julian Morris, John Blundell and Lorraine Mooney have all helped with the research. Funding was provided by the Margaret Laurence Fund, a PERC fellowship, Sir Chips Keswick and the Institute of Economic Affairs.

FOREWORD

In writing this Foreword, I should declare an interest. I am both a keen fly-fisherman and an economist (but no relation to J. R. Hartley of Yellow Pages fame). Some critics regard these as irreconcilable. They fail to understand the immense pleasures generated by fishing: the pleasure of wading in a river on a warm summer's evening (there are other evenings when the English weather is less kind); watching the river come to life with the rising trout; the challenge of trying to fool the trout into taking your artificial fly; and the joy of the catch. I usually confirm the critics' view of the 'madness' of fishing when I return the trout to the river! To economists, fishing is an exercise in constrained maximisation: seeking to maximise the number and size of fish caught subject to the constraints of one rod, one line and one fly. Our club imposes an additional constraint requiring upstream dry fly-fishing only. The late Jack Wiseman had an alternative model of fishing in which he removed all the constraints: his 1944 Normandy model involved throwing a hand grenade into the local river!

Angling offers other opportunities for applying economic analysis. Anglers require clean unpolluted rivers which maximise fish stocks. They find it beneficial to join a club which can afford to rent fisheries and which will have incentives to develop the fishery through restocking and investment in the facilities. Clubs have rules to maintain their fish stocks (for example, restrictions on the numbers of fish which can be killed). But rivers can be, and are, polluted, with pollution destroying the fish stock (and other wildlife dependent on rivers). The pollution can be directly into a club fishery or, more likely, can arise upstream, destroying all river life downstream; or it can arise downstream, preventing the onward passage of migratory salmon and sea trout (for instance, pollution in estuaries). To economists, pollution is an 'externality' and the standard solution is some form of government intervention to 'correct' the market failure and 'improve' the workings of the market. But public-choice analysis suggests that governments can 'fail'. This study of angling conservation uniquely combines economics, law, externalities, property rights and public choice. It is a remarkable story of a voluntary organisation 'solving' the externality problem.

The Anglers' Conservation Association (ACA) is a private-interest self-help group aiming to maintain and improve good-quality rivers in England and Wales. It comprises anglers and others, creating a special-interest group to protect rivers from pollution. Their success in reducing river pollution creates a public good in the form of clean river water which also provides benefits to other river users and consumers (such as walkers and those involved in other water leisure pursuits). The ACA shows how individuals can protect the environment, and it is presented here as 'probably the most efficient pollution-preventing body in Britain' (p. 23).

The actions of the ACA are based on the common law protection of private property rights over water and fishing. 'Where rights are clearly defined, as with anglers and rivers, potential polluters know exactly what they can and cannot do' (p. 107). The ACA is a good example of private actions emerging to 'fill gaps' in legislation (fisheries boards were either inactive or ignored). The idea that anglers should combine to form a special-interest group to finance action using the common law against polluters came from one man – a barrister and angler, John Eastwood, who formed the ACA. It became a pioneering environmental watchdog long before the modern, major environmental groups were created. Typically, the ACA operates by negotiation initially and then court action if necessary (the threat of court action is a deterrent), the aim being to ensure that the 'polluter pays'. Most of the cases never reach the courts, so that ACA is not well known to the public.

Among its successes, ACA lobbying between 1951 and 1985 prevented government legislation from protecting nationalised industries from all liability for pollution. And this study presents many more examples of the 'failures' of government to prevent pollution of the rivers. There are examples of 'capture', with members of regulatory agencies who were potential polluters wishing to avoid the costs of pollution control; governments passing legislation, parts of which were then never implemented; standards complying with effluents (rather than vice versa); and those charged with preventing pollution often being polluters themselves. In 1997, the Environment Agency damaged fishing on a local river through its over-abstraction of water and its rebuilding work. Even more striking is the fact that local authorities are often a major source of pollution (for example, via sewage works). In contrast, industry has demonstrated a willingness to take voluntary action to remedy pollution.

This is a study of a single-issue voluntary-interest group which has achieved success in its campaign against river pollution. The success of the ACA has resulted from its defence of civil rights and its support of individuals and clubs acquiring property rights in the environment in which they pursue their leisure activities. In contrast, government intervention at the national and local levels has all too often been characterised by 'failure', leading to environmental degradation and pollution.

KEITH HARTLEY

Professor of Economics
Centre for Defence Economics, University of York

As in all IEA publications, the views expressed in *Saving Our Streams* are those of the author, not those of the Institute (which has no corporate view), its managing trustees, Academic Advisory Council members or senior staff.

COLIN ROBINSON

Editorial Director, Institute of Economic Affairs
Professor of Economics, University of Surrey
May 2001

PREFACE

Little did I think when my father died at the age of 64 in January 1952 that at the same age, nearly 48 years later, I would be asked to write a Preface to a book about the Anglers' Conservation Association, which he founded five years before his death.

That his vision as a barrister made the ACA possible, and that so many people since have continued to carry the torch for that vision and, like him, have not been scared to take the attack to the polluter's door, is an epitaph of which he would be proud. I am delighted that this book will remind people of the work he did and the organisation he founded.

I always held him in tremendous respect as a father. Like so many who had survived World War I in the trenches, he would never speak about his experiences. He gave great kindness and support to many but expected loyalty and, from his children, complete obedience. He was never lacking in praise if they performed well.

As a fishing companion, his enthusiasm knew no bounds – his excitement at catching a fish was something that was infectious – be it for me, his son, or one of our guests. One such of these was Arthur Ransome, whom I still remember so well, his face wreathed in smiles having caught a salmon just before we had to take him to the station at the end of his stay.

My last day fishing with my father was 16 September 1951, on the River Mawddach in North Wales. It was our ambition to get one more sea trout, or sewin as they were called in Wales, to bring our bag for our holiday up to 60. So nearly did we succeed. I hooked one and lost it, and Father hooked another which came unstuck as he was about to net it. We still remained optimistic, even though the day was drawing to its end, when a shout went up that Father had caught a fish – a grilse – which we landed successfully. But still we needed that sea trout. Another shout went up, and yes, another grilse. Still, a splendid end to our holiday. Was it a premonition as I wrote in my notes, which I now have in front of me, 'A wonderful last day and what may be for ever.' Sadly, it was to prove right. I lost a wonderful fishing companion, but others have since come into my life.

That we still have large areas of unpolluted water is due to a father who had that vision all those years ago to use the common law of the land to help prevent even larger areas of inland water becoming polluted, either by councils or big business. It was cheaper for business to pollute rather than purify the water they used, and sewage works run by councils were low on the list of priorities for upgrading as, unlike today, protection of the environment was not considered to be a vote-winner.

HUGO EASTWOOD

SUMMARY

- Pollution of British rivers increased in the first half of the twentieth century. Private action to clean up rivers and estuaries was taken by the Anglers' Conservation Association (ACA), achieving significant improvement.
- John Eastwood OBE, KC, a barrister and an angler, formed the ACA in 1948 to bring civil suits against polluters who harm fishing. The most common polluters are local authority sewage works, factories and farms.
- Membership of the ACA indemnifies angling clubs and individual fishermen, as potential plaintiffs, against the cost of litigation. This maintenance of cases by a third party is legal because the ACA and the plaintiff have a common interest in preventing pollution of fisheries. The ACA uses traditional English common law.
- Owners or lessees of property bordering a river have certain rights (riparian rights) over the quality and quantity of water in that river. The remedies available are injunction against the polluter and compensation to the riparian owner.
- Only plaintiffs with legal standing (free or leasehold rights or fishing leases) can bring an action. The ACA therefore encourages all anglers and angling clubs to seek property protection by buying stretches of riparian land or acquiring long fishing leases from land owners.

- Since its foundation, the ACA has brought thousands of actions – most famously the 'Pride of Derby' case in 1953, when it cleaned up serious pollution along eight miles of the Derwent and Trent Rivers. The ACA has been awarded hundreds of injunctions and millions of pounds in damages for plaintiffs.
- The ACA has fought multinationals, local authorities and government ministries that have variously tried to attenuate riparian rights and other property rights. The ACA was the only voice to lobby against what would have been the disastrous nationalisation of British rivers.
- The ACA has been a victim of its own success. In trying to avoid the expense of court cases, the ACA is always amenable to settlement – its prime objective is clean rivers, not punitive damages. In fact, most cases end in settlement. Although this is very efficient it brings little public recognition.
- Having benefited from ACA action in the past, many members fall into complacency and fail to renew either their subscriptions to ACA or their leases. Yet the threat from pollution has never disappeared, although now accidents, rather than bad management of effluent, are more likely to be the cause.
- The ACA has never sought the limelight, unlike so many green pressure groups, and only employs a handful of staff to pursue its business. It is the most efficient and determined pollution prevention body in Britain.

1 INTRODUCTION

Pollution of river waters has been the main cause of the
decline of fisheries ... Without the efforts of the ACA,
altogether too many rivers would have become sterile. The
support of the membership and the hard work of
committees, of officers and staff have ensured that the ACA
has been able to campaign vigorously and effectively to
protect the cleanliness and viability of so many of our rivers.
(ACA, 1998: 4)

> HRH Prince Philip, Patron of ACA,
> in the 50th-anniversary *ACA Review*

The quality of the natural environment in England and Wales has
improved enormously over the past fifty years. Government has
been taking action against pollution since 1876, but how much of
the improvement is due to government intervention? Growing environmental awareness has certainly been a significant factor in
cleaning up our countryside, rivers and beaches. But in one particular area, inland rivers, environmental recovery and protection
have been achieved principally by a group of single-minded, self-
ishly motivated private individuals, assisted by a co-operative organisation operating on a shoestring budget and using the ancient
common law as its main tool.

These people are anglers, and their love of fishing is the only
thing that motivates them. Their actions are taken in the civil

courts, using fundamental civil rights laid down by Magna Carta. When they set out to clean up a river they nearly always win, and polluters rarely reoffend. Their activities predate the environmental movement by 25 years, and for at least the first ten years of their existence public opinion was against their work. Apart from never quite having enough money, the greatest obstacle to their successfully ending pollution has often been government bodies or those acting under statutory authority. They have had to protect their common law rights against legislation that has tried to overrule them.

This paper analyses the work of the Anglers' Conservation Association (ACA) in fighting pollution, and so provides an illustration of the legal process. Since its formation in 1948 as a private-interest, self-help group, the ACA has quietly, consistently and successfully fought to improve and maintain good-quality rivers in England and Wales. Its legal actions have established important precedents in environmental protection. It has helped to form policy by providing advice to both Houses of Parliament. The ACA's Director is currently serving on a Task Group to try to solve the huge problem of pollution caused by flooding in disused coal mines.

The basis of its legal actions is very simple. In the common law landowners have certain benefits and duties, called riparian rights, over water flowing across or alongside their land. They cannot own the water, but they can use a 'reasonable' amount of it, and they have the right to a sufficient quality and quantity of water flowing past. Their duties are to ensure that the rights of neighbouring riparian owners are not damaged by their own actions. Furthermore, if the riparian owner has a fishery, he also has the right that migratory fish have free passage up and down the river, from their spawning grounds to the sea.

Adherence to these simple-sounding principles in common law has, in the words of a former Under-Secretary of State for the Environment, Mr Eldon Griffiths, 'been one of the main defences – and sometimes the only defence – against river pollution . . .' (ACA, 1972, volume 19, number 2, p. 21). Nevertheless, during the lifetime of the ACA there have been three attempts to abolish the civil rights of riparian owners through statutory legislation. Fortunately, the ACA and their members mounted successful campaigns to alert MPs, officials and the media, and the rights have remained intact.

In the ACA's history are incidents where a polluting public water authority was successfully sued by a private individual; where an angling club stopped pollution of an estuary forty miles downstream of the club itself; and where ACA lobbying dissuaded government from handing a licence to pollute to large industries. Although they rarely make headlines, ACA cases are hugely influential. Many of its cases are settled by negotiation before they reach the courts – a very efficient process, but one which yields little publicity to or recognition of the ACA as a preventer of pollution.

The ACA is probably the most efficient pollution-preventing body in Britain. This paper details how it has achieved such success, and why its experience demonstrates the error of the idea that individuals either cannot or will not protect the environment.

2 THE ANGLERS' CONSERVATION ASSOCIATION AND THE COMMON LAW

The 1999 annual *ACA Review* reported that 34 legal actions against pollution were being conducted on behalf of members at the beginning of 1999. By the end of the year, this had risen to 42, despite five actions having been won or settled during the year. Damages recovered and passed on to members amounted to £366,890. Halfway through 2000, this success had been trumped by the negotiated settlement of £415,000 in the case of a pollution incident in March 1993. The following report on the River Eden is extracted from the newsletter of the Appleby Angling Association in Westmorland:

> Members will find it only too easy to remember the blackest day in the history of the Club. Few of us thought it would take six long years to gain compensation from the spill of 21,000 litres of ammonium hydroxide fertilizer at a farm on Ploughlands Beck. This led to a lethal slug of this highly toxic substance travelling slowly down the River Eden for more than 14 miles, killing everything in its path. Countless thousands of salmon trout, coarse fish, eels and crayfish lay dead in the water. Next day, piles several feet high littered the banks as they were trawled out.
>
> Our Club lost all its fishing at one stroke. Other clubs suffered too and hotels and guesthouses lost many of the visitors who came to fish the North of England's finest river. The Upper Eden group representing all those affected was

quickly set up, advised and supported by the Anglers' Conservation Association. The ACA, of which we are members, raises money to fight cases like ours on behalf of all who fish. The group's aim has been to make sure that those responsible pay compensation for lost money, lost pleasure and for restocking and restoring the river and its banks and wildlife habitats.

Those who lost most will share compensation amounting to £115,000. In addition, no less than £175,000 will go to a trust fund to be spent on environmental improvement with the full backing of the Environment Agency. Further funds to increase the total will come from other sources. The Club will receive about £50,000 directly to pay for stocking and other expenses and will have a major say in how the money is spent.

It has been a long battle which has involved a lot of effort by the officers and committee of your Club. Their hard work and that of the ACA has at last brought its reward. We look forward to working with others with an interest in the river to make our wild trout fishing once again the best in the North.

This letter from the Appleby anglers neatly describes the work and aims of the ACA. This particular case was unusual in the length of time the litigation took, the extent of the damages, and because it was settled through mediation between the ACA members and the polluters. It is far more common for the ACA to enter into friendly negotiation with polluters, preferably to avoid court action. There was no animosity in this case, but it was complex. It was also the first time a trust fund was set up by anglers to restore and improve the habitat of a river. Damages recovered are usually a few hundred or a few thousand pounds rather than hundreds of thousands, but in each case, the money represents realistic reparation for damage done and, significantly, it goes to the anglers who use it to make good what was lost.

Public opinion puts a high value on environmental protection these days, but even so the Eden case was a difficult one to resolve. After World War II things were very different. The public mood was for economic development, regeneration of industry, building new homes, providing consumer goods and generally making up for the privations of a long and dreary war. Pollution was an occupational hazard of little significance to most people, but it was during this time that the first riparian action against pollution since the nineteenth century was brought.

The early days of the ACA

The River Lea, a tributary of the Thames, was suffering from chronic pollution caused by the Luton Corporation's sewage works in Hertfordshire, north of London. Although the Corporation was complying with the effluent quality objectives (standards considered acceptable to the government of the day), nevertheless pollution resulted as there was not enough water flowing in the river to dilute their effluent. During World War I the Luton Corporation had been producing one million gallons of sewage a day. This was reasonably well diluted by a daily flow of six million gallons of river water. But by 1939, the town of Luton had been greatly developed, with the result that seven million gallons of sewage effluent entered the river every day. The dilution was insufficient and pollution was inevitable, but the Corporation seemingly had statutory authority to continue its actions. That is, it was required by Parliament to accept and treat sewage and the assumption had grown up that such authority covered all the

Corporation's activities in fulfilling their duty. To make matters worse, the sewage works ws new, so there was no hope of improvement being prompted from within the Corporation.

The Lea runs through Brocket Park north of Hatfield in Hertfordshire. Lord Brocket had been a barrister and an MP and had many commercial and charitable interests. Eventually, after years of suffering pollution, he sought remedy in the common law as a riparian owner. The common law of England, as it developed over many centuries, allowed the owner of land adjoining a river or watercourse the entitlement to protect it from pollution and excess abstraction. This entitlement is known as a riparian right. Lord Wensleydale in *Chasemore v. Richards* summarised the law in 1859 as follows:

> The landowner has the right to have water come to him in
> its natural state, in flow, quantity and quality, and to go
> from him without obstruction, upon the same principle that
> he is entitled to the support of his neighbour's soil for his
> own in its natural state. (1859, 7 H.L. Cas. 349)

If a riparian owner's water is polluted by a proprietor higher upstream, he has a good cause of action against the polluter. The remedies available to a sufferer or plaintiff if his case is proven are compensation for loss suffered and the granting of an injunction to restrain any possible future pollution from the same defendant in the action.

The riparian owner also has a right to the ordinary use of the water flowing past his land, that is, to take as much water as is reasonably accepted. However, there is no simple, standard definition of ordinary abstraction. Each case is considered on its own merits, the rule being that extraordinary abstraction that reduces the flow of water is in principle actionable by a lower riparian owner (Wisdom, 1979: 104).[1]

Furthermore, the ownership rights are so strong that it was established in 1867 (*Crossley v. Lightowler*, 1867, 16 L.T. 438) that if a person wished to exercise a riparian right, for instance to stop pollution, it was only necessary for him to own a tiny fraction of the bank of the stream.

Nevertheless, exercising the law is very expensive for individuals and the personal risk is high, because if he loses his case, the plaintiff is liable for all costs – his own and the defendant's. Naturally, this works the other way too – the loser pays for everything. Since the government had made severe pollution that caused a public nuisance a criminal offence in 1876, it was generally assumed that the owners' rights had been superseded, so the use of civil law to bring actions against polluters had all but disappeared in the twentieth century. Lord Brocket put up his own money as plaintiff in a nuisance action, nuisance being a civil wrong or tort. He claimed that his rights had been infringed and that the effluent from the Corporation's sewage works had materially altered the natural state of his water. As a riparian owner, he did not even have to prove that he had suffered damage, only that his water had been affected. A writ was issued and the case of *Lord Brocket v. Luton Corporation* came before Judge Vaisey in 1946. He listened to the evidence, which had been prepared by the embryonic ACA team of solicitor, barrister and expert witnesses, who gave evidence of their analyses. The Corporation as defendants were found liable for polluting the River Lea in Hertfordshire. An in-

---

1   There are several cases which have influenced this position: *Miner v Gilmour*, 1859, 12 Moo. P.C.C. 131; *Norbury (Lord) v. Kitchin*, 1863, 7 L.T. 685; *McCartney v. Londonderry Ry Co.*, 1904, A.C. 301; *White & Sons v. White*, 1906, A.C. 72.

junction was granted and the defendants were also ordered to pay the costs of the action.

Judge Vaisey granted a suspension of the injunction to July 1950 to allow improvements that would stop the pollution. As this date approached and the pollution continued, the defendants applied for further time, even though they admitted that measures taken or planned were still not likely to comply with the injunction. Mr Justice Wynn, who heard the application for a further suspension, pointed out that 'it was no use for the defendants to say that they could not purify their effluent to a higher standard as the Metropolitan Water Board were actually taking this effluent and turning it into drinking water' (ACA, 1950, 1, 4: 89). The judge allowed the defendants a further year on condition that they prepare plans for waterworks treatment of their effluent which could be put out to tender forthwith if the new installation did not stop the pollution.

In retaining the ACA team, Lord Brocket had given them the perfect test of how well their idea would work. For the team the case was 'a try-out against determined opposition and proved its efficiency in action' (ACA, 1950, 1, 1: 10). It showed that it was possible for the ACA to brave conflict or controversy to achieve its goal. It also epitomised many of the cases encountered later – local authorities disregarding common law rights, effluent quality objectives that were useless at preventing pollution, and the lack of dilution for effluents being ignored.

The founder

> Venator:
> Ay, marry Sir, now you talk like an artist and I'll say you are

one when I see you shall perform what you say you can do;
but yet I doubt it.

The Compleat Angler, Isaak Walton

The idea that anglers should group together to finance actions against polluters in the common law came from one man – an angling barrister and Bow Street magistrate. John Eastwood, OBE, KC, analysed the sixteen Acts of Parliament in force in the mid-1940s for the protection of rivers and decided 'that none of them was any good' (ACA, 1953, 5, 1: 65). He saw that the quality of water in a river was highly dependent on how water in that river was used. For example, good salmon fishing could be found on rivers like the Test, which supported little industrial activity, while industrial production near rivers like the Derwent and Trent meant that water quality was far poorer. According to Eastwood, no real effort was apparently being made to stop any polluter from releasing effluent into those British rivers used to support industrial activity. Any statutory action on these industrial rivers had been either ineffectual or even damaging.

Legislation to 1948 – the law and the remedy

The Public Health Act of 1875 made the first attempt to deal with pollution from sewage and gas works, and the Rivers Pollution Prevention Acts (1876–1893) gave local authorities power to take criminal proceedings against polluters. Prior to that, the owner of a river, or of the land adjoining the river, was the only person entitled to protect it from pollution. The Attorney-General could take criminal proceedings only if pollution was so gross as to constitute a public health danger – a public nuisance. 'A public nuisance is an act unwarranted by law or an omission to discharge a legal duty which materially affects the life, health, property, morals or reasonable comfort of a class of citizens, who come within the sphere or neighbourhood of its operation.'[2]

The rights of riparian owners are very strong, and since any offender who ignores an injunction is guilty of contempt of court and can be imprisoned, this means that the private riparian owner is in the strongest possible position to defend his river against pollution. But the cost is the great obstacle to actions.

This Rivers Pollution Prevention Act (1876) attempted to alleviate the expense of private action. However, according to C. Stratton Gerrish, the legal consultant to the ACA from 1950 to 1970, the Act failed because local authorities were only *enabled* to take action to stop pollution and not *obliged* to do so. What is more, the prosecutor under the Act was usually the polluter itself (a local authority) or another local authority. In the case of industrial pollution, the consent for an action had to be given by the Minister of Health, who refused permission if the polluter could demonstrate that there was, as yet, no means of purifying the effluent. The perception following the 1876 Act was that polluters could escape liability if they used the latest technology. The effect of this was that:

> it paid industry handsomely not to discover new methods of effluent treatment. One court, for instance, decided that it was not reasonable to expect any firm to spend more than £100 on purifying its effluent . . . The view became established that it was not their business to do anything unless the pollution was so gross as to create a public nuisance (Gerrish, 1973: 8).

---

2   Sinclair, 1992: 17. Examples of such cases would be: *A-G v. Basingstoke* (1876, 45 L.J. Ch. 726); *A-G v. Lonsdale* (1868, 33 J.P. 534).

Standard of purity

A Royal Commission was established towards the end of the nineteenth century to enquire into the standards of purity of sewage and industrial effluents which ought to be required under the Rivers Pollution Prevention Acts. It recommended in its report of 1912 that a certain standard of purity should be maintained to avoid a public nuisance. Any standard should also allow for the availability of dilution for that effluent. However, the quality of water required to support fish life was not mentioned in the recommendation: sensitive fish like salmon and trout would probably not have survived in water that was polluted but still did not constitute a public nuisance (Gerrish, 1973).

The standard, which became known as the 30/20 standard, called for an effluent with not more than 30 parts per million of suspended solids and not more than 20 parts per million Biological Oxygen Demand (BOD) to be discharged into a receiving water giving at least an eight-to-one dilution factor. According to Gerrish, the Royal Commission's recommendations (although never given statutory effect) were interpreted by local authorities as relieving them of all responsibility for taking action, unless the recommended standards were breached. Both industrial and council polluters therefore considered their effluent to be acceptable as long as it did not infringe these standards.

Biochemical Oxygen Demand is the amount of oxygen needed by micro-organisms to break down organic material. This process takes oxygen out of the water and in gross pollution incidents can deoxygenate a whole stretch of river, killing all living creatures. Dangers to the riverine environment are often found in unlikely places. For example, one pint of milk has a worse BOD effect on a river than 40 gallons of untreated domestic sewage.

Table 1 **Examples of typical Biochemical Oxygen Demand levels**

Pollution type	BOD in mg/litre
Treated domestic sewage	20–60
Raw domestic sewage	300–400
Vegetable washings	500–3,000
Dilute dairy parlour and yard washings	1,000–2,000
Liquid waste draining from slurry stores	1,000–12,000
Liquid sewage sludge	10,000–20,000
Cattle slurry	10,000–20,000
Pig slurry	20,000–30,000
Silage effluent	30,000–80,000
Brewer's grain effluent	30,000–50,000
Milk	140,000

Source: MAFF (1991), Code of Good Agricultural Practice for the Protection of Water.

In this age of environmentalism, it is sometimes hard to imagine what pollution was really like, but a typical case was described in the *ACA Review* in 1959:

> The sewage farm consists of a settlement tank, which does not operate efficiently even in the present drought conditions. After any appreciable rainfall, raw sewage passes over this tank and is piped on to fields over which the liquor flows until it finally runs into a small collecting pond adjacent to Mere Brook. In drought conditions the flow of water in the Brook is very low and was recently found to be overwhelmed by an amount of sewage 10 times as great as the amount of natural water. The worst effect of the effluent is the amount of suspended solid matter which is carried into the Brook in times of rain and eventually settles in a lake belonging to our member where it proceeds to putrefy and create serious nuisance. As the inefficiencies and dangers inherent in this system have been well recognised for many years, the Malvern Urban District Council have been asked whether they will set their house in order

without the necessity for legal action. Their first reaction to this approach has not been encouraging.

Fishery legislation

Government concern about the dwindling salmon populations was aroused back in 1860, with the result that a Commission was appointed to look into salmon fisheries. The Salmon Act of 1861 set down the seasons and methods of taking salmon and created the offence of taking immature and spawning salmon. Coarse fishing was similarly recognised by the Freshwater Fisheries Act of 1878.

By 1923 the legislation had been amended and patched up by eighteen further Acts of Parliament, including the creation of Fishery Boards under the Salmon and Freshwater Fisheries Act of 1907, but still there was no effective protection against pollution. The powers of the Rivers Pollution Prevention Acts (1876–1893), which had previously applied only to sanitary authorities, were extended by the 1907 Act to the new Fishery Boards. This was an improvement in that it removed the conflict of interests arising from a local authority prosecuting itself or a local counterpart – the 'gamekeeper and poacher problem'. Fishery Boards were also given the power by bylaws to regulate the deposit of any matter detrimental to salmon, trout or freshwater fish.

The Salmon and Freshwater Fisheries Act of 1923 consolidated all the previous pieces of legislation and provided some improvements. The defence of best practical means remained but the £100 limit was dropped. The prosecution still had to prove that fish were present when the waters became injurious to fish through the presence of a specific polluting matter directly caused by the accused. The effect of this was to make multiple prosecutions almost impossible – a factory owner could plead that any fish that might have been in a river had already been killed by somebody's else's effluent before he discharged his factory's waste. The Act also gave protection to spawning grounds, spawn and fish food sources. However, the benefits of these changes must have been limited by the continuing need to obtain ministerial consent for an action against mining or manufacturing pollution.

Still, the powers available to Fishery Boards could have been used to great effect. That they were not was largely due to lack of money – some had budgets of as little as £200 a year (£7,600,[3] Carty & Payne, 1998: 36). Successful prosecutions brought only small fines, and their sole source of income was what they could raise by imposing licence duties. Since few anglers would want to buy a licence to fish polluted waters, it follows that the Fishery Boards responsible for the dirtiest rivers also had the least money.

A glimmer of hope

The Public Health Act of 1936 seemed to offer an effective remedy to polluted rivers and a relief to anglers. According to Gerrish (1973), this Act rejected the effluent standard recommendations of the Royal Commission and in effect required sewage effluent to comply with the common law rights of riparian owners.

However, any hope raised was short lived as the Act was modified by the Public Health (Drainage of Trade Premises) Act (1937). This allowed industries to discharge their effluents into sewers (subject to certain safeguards) and threw the onus of purifying them on to the local authorities. In effect, polluters were able to

---

3   Figures in brackets are in 1999 prices (adjusted for inflation).

pump effluents into rivers, as the sewerage system simply could not cope with the volumes and concentration of the discharges.

As Gerrish pointed out in 1960: 'Strangely enough the lamentable amount of pollution existing today is due largely to the various acts of Parliament that have been passed ostensibly to stop pollution' (ACA, 1973: 6).

The crusading angler

John Eastwood wrote in an article for *Country Fair* in 1951 of the 'instinctive love of pure water' which many people felt when gazing at a stream flowing under a bridge. But he thought this enjoyment was spoiled if the bottom of the river was not visible: 'All the pleasure is gone when the water is dead and polluted.' As an angler and barrister, he had pondered the problem for many years. In describing how he set up the ACA, he says that he made two sudden discoveries:

> While pollution was inevitable in Queen Victoria's time, this was no longer the case. During this century science has made such strides that far the greater part of existing pollution can be stopped. This discovery completely alters our sense of values. If a vital industry can get rid of its effluent only by poisoning a river, there seems to be no answer; but, if the effluent can be made harmless, is the industry entitled to destroy the pleasure of millions merely for the sake of cheaper production? An entirely new orientation of rights and duties has thus arisen. There is the relative duty of an industry to its shareholders, or a local authority to its ratepayers, and the wider duty of both to the general public.
>
> My second discovery was this. To all intents and

> purposes every Act of Parliament dealing with pollution is a
> penal Act – that is to say, it creates pollution offences which
> are punishable in a criminal court. There is no Act dealing
> with the civil rights of an injured person. This has never
> been necessary because civil rights are part of the common
> law of the land. They are the basis of freedom, and prescribe
> that an individual shall enjoy what is his without undue
> interference.

He knew that the common law could work, but he was concerned that riparian rights were not being enforced owing to a lack of finance. 'The snag was that the costs of actions to enforce that right would be enormous, because the chief defendants would be great city corporations, nationalised industries and huge combines who'd be bound to fight them every inch of the way' (ACA, 1953, 5, 1: 65). Eastwood wanted to know how to overcome the difficulties of enforcing these rights.

According to his son Hugo (Eastwood, 2000), John Eastwood decided on providing a practical solution when his family's fishing on the River Usk was threatened by a proposed industrial barrage on the river. The water environment he loved might be irrevocably changed and he 'wanted to do something'. He came up with the novel idea of an association designed to spread the risk of an action in common law by raising annual subscriptions among all those with property interest in water to guarantee against legal costs. His correspondence from 1946 showed the first germ of the idea. 'Did I tell you that I have been working on a new scheme to protect our rivers against pollution? It is rather original and aims at enrolling 500,000 anglers on co-operative lines . . . it is my own idea' (D. Eastwood in ACA, 1955, 7, 3: 54).

According to his wife, in the two and a half years prior to the

ACA's formation, John Eastwood wrote three thousand letters (in longhand) to obtain support for the scheme. He also wrote numerous articles, attended many meetings, gave interviews and journeyed all over the country. He hoped to convince other fishermen of his strategy, and to encourage them to follow him. His sincerity and their self-interest would determine the success.

On 6 February 1948 the first meeting of the temporary committee of the Anglers' Co-operative Association was held in a little room in Lincoln's Inn Fields in London's legal district. The ACA was incorporated soon afterwards as ACA Trustee Company Limited. With a Guarantee Fund made up of a £600 (£12,540) float given by the Tackle Makers' Association, and the fees of a modest membership, the ACA was ready to start operations.

It is interesting to note that John Eastwood used the term 'co-operative' to describe his idea. Co-operative (self-help) movements were far more prevalent prior to the formation of the welfare state. At that time it was not unusual for finance for medical care and unemployment insurance to be provided through co-operative associations.[4] It is unlikely that any environmental interest group would use that title today, even though the basis of many environmental ideals is co-operation. In 1994, on merging with the Pure Rivers Society, the co-operative name was dropped in favour of conservation – The Anglers' Conservation Association. What was fundamental to the design of the organisation in 1946 had lost its social relevance.

Eastwood's appeal was not to a notion of public service (that is, a duty to help keep rivers clean, as most environmental groups promote today), but to *all* anglers' self-interest. 'Remember –

---

4   For a detailed assessment of their success, see Green (1994).

every mile of water which is restored to angling means a dozen fewer people competing for your own fishing . . . however sure you may be of your fishing, others have had theirs ruined in next to no time' (ACA, 1950, 1, 1: 7).

He also made it clear in his letters that the ACA would only support common law actions of those riparian owners and angling associations who were paid-up members of the ACA. To be able to free-ride one had to be sure that an ACA member or rich riparian owner (who might litigate) was on the same stretch of river. Eastwood was aware that the incentive to join the ACA would be stronger if he excluded non-members from its benefits. However, he was keen to include other angling associations as he realised the importance of their being members of the ACA. Moreover, the more people who provided the public good of clean river water, the lower the cost to those providing. 'We must co-operate, not only within the association, but also by developing sympathetic partnerships with every other angling organisation great or small' (ibid).

When John Eastwood died on 30 January 1952, obituaries appeared in all major newspapers. Perhaps the most eloquent was the *Birmingham Post*: 'Like Piscator, Eastwood not only "talked like an artist" but performed what he promised . . . The ACA has worked miracles' (*Birmingham Post*, 1952).

3   THE ACA IN ACTION

Some early ACA cases

Riparian rights are all about protection of property, so anybody hoping to exercise these rights must have a legally recognised interest in the property. For angling clubs this means a lease with the riparian landlord, preferably signed under seal, and preferably including a clause in which the riparian owner agrees to be a party in any legal action. Proper leases provide legal standing, but it is important to make them for as long as possible – seven, fourteen or even twenty-one years are suggested by the ACA – for several reasons. On a practical level, a longer lease gives greater incentive for anglers to protect and improve their fisheries. As regards the law, an action is less likely to be brought by a club that only has a year-to-year lease because the only damages that could be recovered if successful would be the loss of a maximum of one year's amenity. A polluted river often takes some years to recover before restocking can be attempted, and a club with a short lease is likely to give up and go elsewhere. Most important is the term of an injunction. This is a court order restraining a polluter for ever. It is appropriate when there is reason to believe that the pollution will continue, and it is strongly enforceable. But 'for ever' actually refers to the term of proprietary interest of the plaintiff. That is why it is best to have the riparian owner as party to an action and why long leases are a better insurance.

The property interest of the riparian owner or angling club is vital to the protection of waterways. Without these bundles of rights, it is doubtful whether the ACA would ever have been formed, or would have been able to act if it had.

River Cynon, Wales

The power of these narrowly defined rights was well illustrated by an early ACA case. Following advice given in the ACA's *Pollution Handbook*, Dr J. R. Steen restored the River Cynon, a 'dead river' in the heart of the Welsh coal-mining valleys, to its former purity. Dr Steen formed the Aberdare and District Anglers' Association and obtained over thirty seven-year leases which covered the whole river. With some preliminary advice from the ACA, the anglers of Aberdare set about stopping the discharge of gas liquor by the Gas Board and the pollution with coal slurry by the Coal Board, and caused a filter to be built to remove coal dust from the river. The Aberdare Urban District Council gave assurances that sewage pollution would cease, and other smaller sources of pollution were also cleaned up. In 1950, the Co-operative Wholesale Society had proposed discharging chlorinated water into the river, but back-pedalled after hearing from the ACA solicitors.

Not all anglers were so inspired, though. According to Dick Hodges (2000), a member of the ACA executive since the mid-1950s, many angling clubs were nervous about joining the ACA in the early days because they perceived the organisation as a threat to them and hence many did not heed its advice. 'They didn't seem to realise that they could lose everything if they didn't pay to join ACA,' a bemused Hodges concluded. Still, John Eastwood's hope of enrolling half a million members is a distant one. Membership in 2000 was edging towards 16,000 and recruitment is a constant struggle, which makes the ACA's achievements all the more remarkable.

River Cray, Kent

The first case to be entirely handled and financed by the ACA was *Orpington and District Angling Association v. Vegetable Parchment Mills Ltd*. In March 1948 all the fish in the club's lake at St Mary Cray in Kent were killed. The ACA experts identified the cause as sulphuric acid discharged from the defendants' mills into the River Cray, which filled the club's lake. The anglers were successful and eventually received £1,250 (£26,125) in damages, which was handed over to the club secretary with great ceremony by John Eastwood himself.

Having stressed above the importance of a proper fishing lease, it is interesting that the Orpington club had no fishing lease at all. They rented the land on a verbal tenancy and fished from the land. Neither did they have the right to fill their lake from the River Cray. The ACA must have been very relieved to win the case for the member and recover all their own costs. Gerrish mentioned several years later that 'few of our members realised how near the ACA was to crashing before it ever became airborne . . . the only way to save [the ACA] was to produce some tangible results, so the first action sponsored by the ACA was started and, by the mercy of providence, won with the backing of a fighting fund of just £200' (£4,180, ACA, 1967, 16, 9: 15).

However, the ACA was happy to report in May 1950 that it had 'won eight contested High Court actions in six months and in as many more cases the required result was obtained without even having to start legal proceedings'. Moreover, the many polluters who had 'snapped their fingers at Fishery Boards and Public Health Authorities for years, have thrown in their hands as soon as a riparian owner's action has been started against them'.

River Gade, Middlesex

One defendant in an early case did fight, and they were a £12 million-a-year (£242 million) paper milling concern. The case was an important one because large stretches of waterways were concerned. In *Elms Angling Club Ltd v. J. Dickinson & Co Ltd* (1949), the pollution alleged by the plaintiffs had already been the subject of a report by the Ministry of Agriculture and Fisheries in 1932, and many subsequent complaints had been made. Penal proceedings had been taken in 1939 but the Watford Bench had refused to convict. The defendants denied any pollution of the River Gade, so a trial was inevitable. The ACA Trustees Co. Ltd gave the plaintiffs an unlimited indemnity in respect of costs, although this must have caused some anxiety since the case was expected to last for two or three weeks and the costs to run into several thousand pounds.

In the event, the defendants folded during the opening speech of Mr G. R. Upjohn, KC, the ACA counsel, and submitted to an injunction and costs. The plaintiffs had been joined by many other angling clubs affected by the pollution, which the Thames Conservancy stated had affected the River Colne and the Grand Union Canal as far as Uxbridge. Altogether, forty miles of waterways stood to benefit from the removal of the pollution.

During the course of the hearing, Mr Justice Vaisey commented on the most unsatisfactory state of affairs in which Parliament had set up boards with responsibility for preventing river pollution but had failed to give them adequate powers, with the result that 'public spirited individuals have to undertake the enormous financial risks of civil proceedings to deal with such cases as this'.

River Torridge, Devon

A case which presented the ACA experts with great technical difficulties, again with long-standing and composite pollution, was of the River Torridge in north Devon. The Borough of Great Torrington was founded over a thousand years ago by Alfred the Great, who, like those who followed him, had made no provision for sewage disposal, and the river was being polluted by both sewage and milk factory effluent.

Murmurs of pollution issuing from Torridge Vale Dairies Ltd first emerged in the 1920s. Then it was just a small cheese and butter producer but, as the town grew, so did the dairy. It was considerably enlarged in 1932, and the ditch into which the factory waste and sewage was poured became seriously polluted. Yet despite an abominable stench and thousands of fish killed in the Torridge, into which the ditch flowed, the Fishery Board analysis of the water revealed a perfectly satisfactory report – BOD figures being around 0.1 and 0.2. They could find no evidence of pollution and assumed that their samples were always taken too late. Several public inquiries were held about proposals for a sewage works, and a riparian action was started but abandoned on the outbreak of war in 1939. The absence of scientific evidence would have scuppered the riparian action and possibly persuaded the townsfolk that £8,000 (£157,700) was too much to spend on a sewage works. (Ten years later, this cost had risen to £50,000 (£665,605).)

The Fishery Board and County Council had been trying to stop the pollution for many years. The case was finally brought to the notice of the ACA by Colonel J. T. Upton, one of its founder members. The ACA and Colonel Upton decided to proceed without chemical evidence on the footing that a river that smelled and frothed was not in its natural state of purity. Two writs were issued in December 1948 against the Corporation and the dairy company, claiming in each case an injunction and damages. The Corporation delivered no defence to the plaintiff's statement of claim and agreed to submit to an injunction. The dairy company, however, delivered a defence in which they admitted pollution but claimed that it was only slight and intermittent and did no harm.

The ACA Trustee Company gave the plaintiff an unlimited indemnity in respect of both actions. To its credit, and as testimony to good relations, the Fishery Board raised a special guarantee fund, underwritten by riparian owners in their district, to assist the ACA. The action was conducted by the ACA solicitor, counsel and experts.

ACA experts continued with their chemical analysis in the hope of discovering what was going on. They stumbled on the answer when one sample was wrongly taken. Rather than collecting water from below the surface in the normal way, it included a considerable sample of the surface film of water. The effluent from the milk factory contained considerable quantities of milk and milk fat mixed with a very large volume of hot condenser water. The effluent complied with the Royal Commission standards of dilution, but, as soon as it entered the water, the fat separated and formed a surface film over the river which very soon began to putrefy, form disgusting masses of froth and create objectionable smells. The surface film of fat probably hindered oxygenation of the water and, being animal fat, which is not iridescent on water, it was invisible.

This case shows the determination and industry of the ACA experts but, more seriously, it exposes the danger of relying on effluent quality standards. An authority taking samples in the proper manner and applying the proper standards would have no evidence on which to bring a prosecution. The Torrington case set a standard that alarmed local authorities and polluting industries. The judge stated that 'the duty of anyone who turns effluent into a stream is to regulate his discharge so that it does not pollute the stream ... The real test is whether pollution occurs when the flow of the stream is at its minimum and when the discharge of effluent is at its maximum volume and worst quality' (ACA, 1951).

A rare defeat

The ACA suffered its first defeat in *Stokoe v. Shand Ltd*, a pollution case on 28 March 1966. Cyanide releases from the defendant's premises resulted in 1962/3 in a series of fish kills on the River Axe. Initially, the case was settled by negotiation, with the defendant compensating the ACA members and assuring them that he had taken additional precautions to prevent further escape of cyanide. However, within a few weeks there was another heavy killing of fish caused by a cyanide release from the defendant's premises, which convinced the ACA committee that it was useless to rely on promises to reform. As the defendant had also been prosecuted by the Devon River Board a writ was issued claiming an injunction. The defendant admitted responsibility but said he had made alterations which would make it impossible for more cyanide to escape. The judge decided against an injunction but kept the case open and gave the plaintiff leave to apply to the court for an immediate injunction if there was another incident.

In August 1965 another fish kill caused by cyanide occurred downstream from the defendant's factory. The ACA pursued the action despite knowing that it would be difficult to prove that the cyanide originated from the defendant's factory. It was hoped that even if it were not possible to prove how the cyanide had been discharged into the river, it would be possible to apply the rule in *Rylands v. Fletcher* (1868). Under this rule, the ACA might satisfy the court that large quantities of cyanide were being stored by the defendants without satisfactory safeguards and that they must be held responsible if any of it went astray (ACA, 1966, 16, 6: 11). This celebrated rule, which has been held to apply whether the things brought on to land be 'beasts, water, filth or stenches', states that:

> Where a person for his own purposes brings and keeps on
> land in his occupation anything likely to do mischief if it
> escapes, he must keep it at his peril, and if he fails to do so
> he is liable for all damage naturally accruing from the
> escape. (Smith & Keenan, 1979)

The defendants denied that the cyanide had come from their factory and suggested that the poisoning of the river must have been the work of poachers or saboteurs.

At the trial the judge rejected this alternative theory and was, according to the ACA, satisfied that the cyanide could only have come from the defendant's premises, but there was absolutely no evidence to show how it had got into the river. A court order against 'causing or permitting' harm was not broken merely by the defendant pursuing a course of action which was certain to lead to a breach of the order or covenant. To enable the court to interfere there must be some direct action by the defendant in breach of the order.

As the ACA was only making an application under the order obtained previously, the costs involved to the Association were not anything like as great as would have been incurred in a full-scale action, but at the same time they were not trifling. 'The one redeeming feature is that in the course of the hearing the defendant's Counsel announced that in January the defendant had decided to discontinue the use of cyanide altogether for hardening steel and to adopt a new process which will not involve any discharge of effluent to the river' (ACA, 1966, 16, 6: 11). This rare case, where the ACA took a chance and lost, serves as an illustration and reminder of the importance of being certain of evidence and establishing causation that satisfies the law.

Monitoring pollution

The ACA is meticulous in gathering evidence so that it can be very certain of its case before considering taking action. It is also anxious to avoid court action where possible and always offers negotiation. These are prudent measures, which on balance save money, but they also mean that the threat of action is not an empty one and that relations are kept as friendly as possible. The ACA once received a letter thanking it for its helpful suggestions and 'for the courteous manner in which you received us on Tuesday' (ACA, 1950, 1, 3: 58). The writers were the defendants, and Tuesday was the day on which the ACA had obtained an injunction against them.

The many experts used by the ACA in investigations include chemical analysts, biologists, engineers, photographers (terrestrial and aerial) and advisers on rehabilitation and restocking of water. One of the great strengths of the ACA method is that anglers are their own watchdogs. Over the years the ACA has trained volunteer anglers to become Water Pollution Officers for their clubs. The *ACA Pollution Handbook* gives detailed instructions on how to take samples of what might be polluted waters and get them sent off safely and quickly for analysis. This is especially useful in the case of sudden pollution, or accidents. Anglers are advised to note exactly where the incident occurred, at what time and, if necessary, to chase the wave of pollution downstream and take a sample in their gumboots or Thermos flask if they have nothing else to hand.

In 1990 the then Director, Allen Edwards, announced that he had negotiated a discount for ACA members using the Anglers' Analytical Service, whereby the pH value, nitrate, sulphate and ammonia levels and the Biochemical Oxygen Demand (BOD) could be determined for a total of £21. It also offered to test for many other substances, and provided a home BOD testing kit for £14. Not only that, but the company offered to donate 10 per cent of the income derived from basic river quality analysis to the ACA to help fight for improved river quality.

Pollutants not necessarily toxic

Many pollutions are caused by substances that are not toxic but have simply overwhelmed the receiving environment. In a bizarre incident in 1977, when an articulated tanker turned over on a bridge, its contents – 1,000 gallons of orange juice – managed to ruin two miles of excellent trout fishing.

In 1997 there was a fish kill caused by sugar syrup escaping from a cider factory; in 1999 fishing was repeatedly spoiled by soil entering the river from a carrot washing factory. Roadworks or in-river works which send down suspended solids are a perennial problem. Although seemingly innocuous, they cause discoloration, poor visibility and settle out on the riverbed, spoiling spawning grounds.

The first ACA case against a gravel washing operation, Redmires Sand and Ganister, in 1951 on the River Wear in north-east England, brought both support from all the other sand and gravel concerns in the area to help defend the action, and a rash of similar cases: 'It would seem that the case of the Wear has made many people realise that they have been putting up with this sort of nuisance unnecessarily' (ACA, 1954, 5, 3: 59). Complaints had been made against many of these concerns by the Fishery Board, but they had all been ignored. This case is also interesting in showing how injunctions work, especially since the defendants had previously shown such disregard for the nuisance they were causing.

The company was digging and washing gravel on the banks of the river and even on the riverbed. The 'solids in suspension' were washed down and were clogging the shallows of the River Wear, leading to an explosion of algae and death to fish and insect life. The defendant's activity was enjoined for physically polluting the Wear.

However, two years later the company was again polluting the river in breach of its injunction. Immediate proceedings were brought and the court heard that the plaintiff's water was heavily discoloured and made turbid as a result of the defendants working a mechanical dragline in the river and driving a fleet of lorries back and forth across the riverbed to be loaded with gravel. As the defendants admitted the offence and apologised, Mr Justice Vaisey decided against committing them to prison. He was concerned to clear up a misapprehension which had emerged from the defendant's affidavit. It seemed that the defendant had thought that his injunction applied only to pollution caused in a particular way, and that he was free to find other methods of pollution. The judge strongly emphasised that such orders demanded absolute obedience. No further complaint was made.

ACA Trustees Co. Ltd and the Guarantee Fund

The Guarantee Fund acts like an insurance policy against loss incurred by plaintiffs through unsuccessful litigations. As with all insurance, the risk is spread as wide as possible so that individual participators do not have to bear a disproportionate liability. The fund is voluntary with a few large donors, but any sum is welcomed. Class 4F2 from a school in Surrey raised £14 in 1973 'by the girls holding a coffee morning, selling their own cakes, and the boys having a sponsored litter collection, which also cleaned up our school grounds'.

But not all the costs incurred in presenting cases are recovered, so the trustees have to consider carefully which cases to support.

The ACA Trustee Company Limited has two outstanding objectives. The first is to use the Guarantee Fund to spread the liability of individual members taking actions against polluters. The second is to step in and act as trustee for any club where club members are nervous about accepting the risk of becoming trustees themselves.

There are strong advantages in a club's taking out a proper lease under seal as it strengthens the club's claim should any pollution occur. As mentioned above, a club with a long lease has a greater claim for damages. Similarly, any injunction granted will run only for the period of the lease, which is why it is always preferable that the property owner is party to the case. The landlord is guaranteed his rent, and the club has a certain number of years' fishing at a fixed rate and a greater incentive to protect and improve its water.

However, if the club defaulted on its rent or injured the landlord in some way, the trustees might be individually liable. If a lawsuit were necessary, the trustees would have to be a party to the action, and they would be personally liable for the costs. To remove this risk to an individual fisherman, the ACA Trustee Co. Ltd will act as trustee and hold the lease on behalf of the club, and in the event of litigation the company is the plaintiff.

The extreme patience, diligence and financial resources required when going to law are well illustrated in the case where the ACA acted on behalf of the Burton Mutual Angling Association in *ACA Trustees Co. Ltd and Others v. Thomas Bolton & Sons Ltd* (1951). The Dove and Churnet rivers had been described in a publication from the British Field Sports Society in 1950 as the site of one of the most devastating pollutions in the country. The real difficulty of the case was said to be that, even if the pollution could be stopped, the 'riverbed and banks have become so saturated with poison that it may take years for the river to clean itself'. Once the case was reported in the *ACA Review*, several other riparian owners aligned themselves with the ACA Trustee Co. Ltd. When the case was brought, the defendants, who had copper plating mills at Froghall and Oakamoor, offered no defence to the charge of polluting the River Dove with copper. An injunction was granted and two years later fish had returned but were still not breeding properly. It was thought that as the river had been dead for twenty or thirty years, old deposits of copper might still be leaching from the riverbed. It was also known that copper was only one of the pollutants present, so the ACA authorised an investigation to discover the exact nature of the pollution and how the Dove and Churnet might be cleaned up.

Although the River Dove and the Churnet above the town of Leek recovered and provided excellent fishing, the stretch of the Churnet below the town to its mouth remained virtually dead owing to organic pollution. After spending six years and £1,500 (£21,620) on investigations, the ACA found three sources responsible: the Corporation sewage works, a paper mill and a dye works.

The Trent River Board was acting concurrently with these investigations to apply pressure to the wrongdoers, and in the event all the pollutions were stopped without a court case. The Leek Corporation reconstructed its sewage works to cope with trade waste, to include the dye works' waste, as well as domestic sewage. The situation of the paper mill was very different. Although its effluent complied with the standard required by the river board, there was not sufficient diluting water available to avoid pollution. The firm decided to go beyond the authority standard and comply with the common law requirement of a clean river. The ACA speculated that the firm was mindful of its action against the copper works and had seen the ACA experts in the vicinity with their bottles and nets and decided to take pre-emptive action. The ACA could have recovered costs from the company, but considered that, since it was trying hard to achieve the desirable result, and that large stretches of Midlands rivers had been cleaned up and were fit for fishing, the money was well spent.

After twelve years, the Burton anglers were rewarded, but they must have been relieved that they were spared the responsibility of carrying the case to its conclusion.

Criminal or civil?

Most people have a vague idea that government bodies, such as the Environment Agency today and its predecessors, exist to monitor pollution and to bring prosecutions that result in fines. Few will be familiar with their ancient, individual civil rights under the common law, and fewer still will know of riparian rights to restrain pollution. Even the informed might wonder what the point is when the government body is there.

An offender may learn his lesson, or he may pay the fine and carry on as before. In criminal law the prosecution must start again and bring another summons in the magistrates' court. This is an expensive and time-consuming process. The fine imposed may cover the costs of the prosecution, but is paid to the Exchequer. In the case of a river pollution that kills fish, it may be that the water is so bad that the anglers and other recreational users have given up and gone elsewhere, so the Agency may consider that the public benefit in bringing a prosecution is outweighed by the cost.

A civil claim, brought in a civil court, either the county court or the High Court, is an entirely different matter. It is a claim by an individual to prevent a pollution, and it may be brought before actual damage is done (*quia timet* – 'because he fears'). If brought after the damage is done, compensation may be claimed as well. If it seems that the pollution will recur, the polluter can be restrained from pollution by an order of the court – an injunction. These cases can only be brought by the individuals whose property is affected.

From the fisherman's point of view, the important thing is that the order of the court to stop the pollution is permanent. It lasts for as long as the person bringing the action, the plaintiff, has an interest in the property. Not only must the pollution cease, but it must never be started again. If the pollution does continue, the polluter is in contempt of court, can be imprisoned and have his property sequestrated, and will be required to pay the sufferer compensation for continuing pollution. These drastic powers are rarely used, but the threat of them is real. A court will suspend injunctions against industrial polluters if they can show they are making a proper effort to put things right.

Lenient but strict

The court will generally allow those bodies with statutory authority to deal with sewage a reasonable time to improve their technology, but with a definite understanding that action must be taken and the pollution stopped. To be seen to be trying hard but achieving nothing will not do.

In *Astor and Another v. Sevenoaks Rural District Council* (1954) the defendants were allowed to continue polluting the River Eden in Kent with sewage for another two years to allow them to build a new sewage works at Edenbridge. When the time was up, the council asked for a further suspension of the injunction for one year, claiming that the work was being held up by the Minister of Housing and Local Government and by the plans to build a new housing and industrial estate on the outskirts of Edenbridge. As it stood, the council's surveyor had not even started to design the new sewage works because he did not know the specification.

Mr Justice Danckwerts stated that the council appeared to have dealt with the matter in a most perfunctory and thoroughly unsatisfactory manner. His Lordship was prepared to give no more than three months' extra time. He suggested that the matter would probably move a great deal quicker if members of the council realised that they might be sent to prison if the judge thought they had been unduly negligent or not sufficiently diligent in pressing the minister for quicker action. In the meantime the council had to pay the costs of the application and continuing damages to the plaintiff.

4 LANDMARK CASES

Pride of Derby
(Pride of Derby and Derbyshire Angling Association Ltd and Earl of Harrington v. British Celanese Ltd, the Derby Corporation, the British Electricity Authority, 1952)

The ACA's most famous case is usually referred to simply as the Pride of Derby, after the angling club involved (1952, 1 All ER 179; Court of Appeal, 1953, 1 All ER 1326). It established the ACA's reputation and later alerted the author to the existence of the ACA. It involved a major multiple pollution of the River Derwent, eight miles of which was dead, as was three miles of the River Trent into which it flowed. The water flowing past the plaintiff's property was 'black, opaque, hot and stinking; the bottom was carpeted with sewage fungus and the temperature of the water was extremely high – often between 90° and 95°F. In summer it was completely deoxygenated' (ACA, 1952, 3, 2: 27). In 1942, salmon were still running up the river below Derby, but when the ACA team investigated ten years later, the only life in the river was mosquito larvae. When the Fishery Board turned a consignment of roach into the river in November 1950, the fish died within a few minutes.

The plaintiff's case was that the dry-weather flow of the Derwent below Derby was about 100 million gallons per day, of which British Celanese Ltd were extracting 72 million gallons. The Derby

Corporation and British Celanese were discharging effluent amounting to 80 million gallons a day – all bad effluents, into the bargain. The Derby sewage works was overloaded. Having been built in 1906 and enlarged (following an adverse government report) in 1933 to treat 6 million gallons a day, in 1950 it was treating, or failing to treat, 9.5 million gallons a day. According to its own analysis, the works rarely achieved more than 50 per cent purification, while often it was under 20 per cent. The British Electricity Authority's role in the affair was to take the results and heat them. This 'Hell's Brew', as the plaintiffs' counsel called it, made the river hotter than the Red Sea. Even tropical fish could not have survived in it.

Before the trial opened, British Celanese Ltd withdrew its defence and asked only that the inevitable injunction be suspended. After listening to the evidence for nearly two days, the remaining defendants admitted that the plaintiff's water was substantially polluted, but the Corporation denied that their sewage had anything to do with it and the British Electricity Authority (BEA) contended that the high temperature was beneficial to fish and assisted them in spawning.

Apart from these defences, both the BEA and the Derby Corporation claimed that their special statutory powers could override the common law, in effect claiming that they were entitled to pollute the river. BEA admitted that its power station had been enlarged until it was too big for the river. The surveyor to the Derby Corporation stated that he had first reported the overloaded and unsatisfactory state of the sewage works in 1946, but that no plan had been drawn up until three months after the commencement of the ACA action. Defending counsel argued that, provided the sewage works was properly constructed originally, the local authority could not be compelled to enlarge or improve it because the population had increased, nor to keep it running efficiently, and so could not be answerable to a riparian owner if its works were overloaded.

Mr Justice Harman found against all the defendants and issued injunctions against them all. He found that neither the Corporation nor the BEA had proven prescription by their private statutes. During his judgment he said that a distressing feature of the case was the inactivity of the Fishery Board, which, in spite of the obvious facts, apparent for many years, had done nothing.

Interestingly, the ACA's experts were refused access to local authority land to investigate the source of the Derby Corporation's pollution, partly because the report from the Trent Fishery Board claimed that there was no 'culpable pollution in respect of which they had any power of action'. The Derby Corporation felt that, as there was no action taken against them for public nuisance, they should not be sued for private nuisance. In an attempt to gather evidence to prove them wrong, two ACA experts went to considerable lengths. They just avoided being sucked into an intake pipe, climbed trees to get better views of the pollution, were shipwrecked and finally took photos from the air to prove their case. In fact, they took whatever action they could within the law.

Nevertheless, the issue was not resolved immediately. Both Derby Corporation and British Electricity appealed the ruling, which was heard by the Master of the Rolls, Lord Evershed, Lord Justice Denning and Lord Justice Romer in the Court of Appeal in December 1953. In his judgment, the Master of the Rolls said that Derby Corporation's appeal rested on two points. The first was that, if they acted within the Derby Corporation Acts of 1907 and 1930, the plaintiff had no cause of action. The second was that, even if the plaintiff did have a cause of action, no injunction ought ever to be granted against the Derby Corporation or any local authority in respect of sewage pollution, and that to do so was an improper interference with the Minister of Housing and Local Government and an impudent invasion of the sovereign authority of the Derby Corporation. The Master of the Rolls said he was shocked at the suggestion that it was improper for the plaintiffs to ask for protection in Her Majesty's courts. Defendant's counsel withdrew the suggestion and agreed that it should not have been made. His Lordship also refused to consider the suggestion that, since it would cost a lot of money to stop the pollution and the plaintiff's fishing had a low value, the court ought to exercise its discretion and refuse an injunction.

His Lordship came to the conclusion, which became a highly influential precedent, that the Derby Corporation Acts expressly prohibited the defendants from causing a nuisance. Only a private statute that specifically authorised pollution could override the common law. He found that the wholly admirable judgment of Mr Justice Harman was correct in every particular: the appeal failed and was dismissed, with costs.

The BEA appealed for a variation in terms of the injunction. Since it had a statutory right to return hot water to the river so long as it did not damage the fish, it asked whether it might not reduce the temperature to suit the fish, rather than to cool it completely. His Lordship agreed to limit the injunction, but gave the Earl of Harrington leave to apply for restoration of the full injunction if in the future he should want to use the river for other purposes.

By 1956 Derby Corporation still had not properly updated its sewage works, and because of the increased sewage and decay to its facilities, the costs of compliance were estimated to have been fourfold greater than had they done the work in 1952 (ACA, 1967, 16, 9: 15). All the defendants asked for repeated suspensions of their injunctions. In fact, British Celanese had managed to remove the worst of its pollution very quickly, simply by cleaning its drains and overhauling the purification plant that had fallen derelict during the war. The last injunction came into force in 1958.

Reviewing the case fifteen years later, C. Stratton Gerrish revealed that 'if British Celanese Limited, the first defendants in the Derby case, had not thrown their hands in when they did the ACA would have had to drop the case as the guarantee fund was then insufficient to cover the costs of a prolonged trial against three defendants' (ACA, 1967, 6, 9: 15). 'The case lasted seventeen days, still the longest of all the ACA legal battles' (ACA, 1988: 25).

The success of the Pride of Derby case has had lasting effects. In 1980, the Secretary of Derbyshire County Council Angling Club had to turn away six hundred applications for season tickets and refuse hundreds of applications for angling matches on this very stretch of river. 'The match-angling ace, Ivan Marks, said that the Lower Derwent is the best angling venue in England' (ACA, 1980).

Now the area along the south bank of the Lower Derwent is a park and nature trail, created and maintained by Derby City Council and supported by Acordis (formerly British Celanese). Acordis still extracts 204 million litres (45 million gallons) a day for cooling from its settling lakes. After use, a small amount goes to Severn Trent Water's treatment plant and the rest is returned directly to the river. There are many factories and works on the north side of the river, including Rolls-Royce plc. The power plant farther down the river is recognisable by its cluster of cooling towers. The river is now healthy and supports chub, dace, gudgeon, perch, pike, roach and barbel. The park and river trail are a considerable civic amenity, and the private nature reserve owned and run by Acordis, and even Severn Trent's sludge lagoons, provide a livelihood for a variety of wildlife. Nowadays, anglers are outnumbered by cyclists and dog walkers, but if the ACA had not succeeded in stopping pollution when it did, the river and its environs might have deteriorated further, with these new amenities not yet provided.

Case mix and advisory role

During the Pride of Derby case, the ACA received a lot of attention in the press, some of it 'rather wild and woolly'. The *ACA Review* put the record straight with a full account of its activities up to that point. In all, 192 cases of pollution or anticipated pollution had been referred to the ACA. Most often, members wanted only advice, and the ACA was asked to take action in only 35. Of these, eight could not be pursued because the member had no legal title and his landlord would not co-operate – in most cases the landlord was the Docks and Inland Waterways Executive. In four cases 'we came to the conclusion after investigation that the member's claim was bogus or completely trivial'. Fifteen cases were dealt with without legal action; eight were continuing pollutions which were stopped and seven were non-recurring pollution in which compensation was paid to the injured party. Writs were issued in 22 cases against 25 defendants. Of these, '13 threw their hands in almost as soon as a writ was issued; 6 submitted to judgment in later stages before trial and only 6 actually let the matter come into Court' (ACA, 1952, 3, 3: 37). During preparation for the Pride of Derby case, the ACA Committee was very careful with its resources, knowing that the case could take most of its energy and all its Guarantee Fund, and so cases were probably building up.

The Myddelton case (see below) followed soon after the Pride of Derby and is a landmark case because it tackled the vexed question as to what the common law could do about estuarial pollution.

Estuaries

Pollution of the sea coast and estuaries in 1950 was 'appalling', according to a study from the British Field Sports Association, despite the vigorous tidal action around the coasts. However, it was established in Magna Carta that all tidal rivers are for the benefit of all members of the public, and only inland rivers and streams are subject to private ownership rights. This left the ACA with no direct course of action to help struggling sea anglers, except insofar as reducing pollution in a river also reduces pollution reaching an estuary. However, the ACA's solicitor knew of a possible cause of action in that polluted salt water prevents the exit and return of migratory fish – an infringement of the common law rights of the fishery owner.

An important new decision had been made in the case of *Nicholl and Others v. Penybont Main Sewerage Board* (1951) in which Mr R. I. Nicholl and the Ogmore Angling Association had obtained an injunction against the discharge of untreated sewage into the Ogmore below Bridgend in South Wales. The significance of this was that the anglers were lessees of the fishing rights on the river for eight miles above the source of pollution: the pollution was preventing the free passage of sea trout and other migratory fish up the river. Despite this decision, there were other grounds of action against the defendants (discharge of raw sewage being illegal under the Public Health Act), so the issue of the free passage of fish was not fully argued. Moreover, the site of the pollution was in the freshwater part of the river.

Myddelton and Others v. J. Summers and Sons Ltd, 1953

Colonel Myddelton claimed that salmon smolts were being killed in the River Dee estuary in Wales, and his fishery, 35 to 40 miles upstream, was being harmed. The only cause of action was the obstruction of the free movement of fish between their spawning ground and the sea. The ACA knew this would be an important case and asked for increased guarantees from its members in case the action took a long time to present. Counter-guarantees were put up by the netsmen of the Dee estuary, who were losing their livelihood because of estuarial pollution.

Colonel Myddelton had previously, and largely at his own expense, managed to restrain Monsanto Chemicals Ltd from polluting farther up the river. The case had been strongly contested. (It was on this case that John Eastwood was working when he died in 1952.) But cleaning the tidal estuary was the key to restoring the river.

At that time, local authorities and industrialists had come to assume that pollution of tidal waters was permissible. In fact, polluters could have been prosecuted under the Salmon and Freshwater Fisheries Act of 1923, but there was great difficulty in proving an offence under this Act in the case of multiple pollution. The pollutants in the estuary were being washed back and forth by the tide, and determining which was discharged by whom and which caused the mischief was impossible. The common law has no such difficulty with multiple pollution, as the liability of a number of polluters is joint and several – the injured party can sue any one or more of them for full reparation of damage. It is not necessary to apportion or evaluate the blame or liability between them. The polluter cannot escape liability by proving that someone else was also polluting the river.

This case was important to all anglers because many estuaries had suffered from this lack of control: migratory fish were almost extinct in the Tyne and Tees and were being obstructed by pollution in the estuaries of the Usk, Severn, Wyre, Taw and Torridge.

Mr Justice Roxburgh found that cyanide pollution by the defendant, J. Summers and Sons Limited, created a material obstruction to the free passage of salmon through the estuary. This pollution was an interference with the right of the fishery owners on the river and thus 'there should be judgment for the plaintiff in the form of an injunction and damages'. In the event, it took only two months to solve the problem. A new closed-circuit cooling system was installed which prevented the escape of cyanide into the Dee estuary. Although this cost the company £6,000 (£86,482), and would have been cheaper if built in at the outset, it was probably not too great an inconvenience for a large plant to sustain.

That most trouble in estuaries could have been prevented quite easily with proper control and forethought was noted by the ACA, but at the same time it saw no cause for 'rushing headlong into an irresponsible witch hunt among polluters of estuaries'. Even so, it did expect to see the polluters start 'setting their houses in order'. But while industry had 'shown itself anxious to play its part in Britain's clean-the-rivers campaign' (*Reader's Digest*, March 1959), it soon became clear that local authority sewage works posed a far more intractable problem.

The Ribble Fisheries' Association organised a public meeting at Preston, Lancashire, in November 1958 to protest against the disgusting and deteriorating state of the Ribble estuary. The meeting was well supported. Local MPs, the Mayor of Wigan, the Medical Officer of Health and ACA experts were among those who gave speeches. A string of resolutions was passed, 'not only unanimously but with acclamation', to urge action from the Lancashire River Board, and these were copied to the Home Secretary, government ministers and local MPs. Specifically, the resolutions named the culprits – seven sewage works, the Gas Board and the UK Atomic Authority.

> These authorities and public bodies are called upon to instal
> proper treatment and purification plant without further
> delay, and put an end once and for all to their present
> practices, which are more in keeping with the Middle Ages.
> (ACA, 1959, 10, 1: 2)

The ACA Editor's comment on the meeting is also revealing:

> We do feel that a well-organised meeting of this kind can
> often do more for the causes which all of us have so much at
> heart than any amount of legal action. A meeting of this sort
> does a great deal to arouse the public conscience which, on
> the subject of river pollution, has been atrophied for far too
> long.

However, the Editor also drew attention to the credit squeeze that had been applied to government spending and the reluctance of ratepayers to pay for the works. The difficulties of obtaining funds and apportioning responsibility in the public sector were apparent in the report of a long-running action on the River Culm in Devon. 'There is now every expectation that the river will be completely free from pollution within a very few years. This end could have been achieved much earlier but for the bickering between the Authorities concerned with sewage disposal in the area.'

In the case of the Ribble, the Lancashire River Board took the initiative, and its annual report for 1962 was featured in the *ACA Review*: 106 sewage works had been built or reconstructed, new sewers laid, trade effluents connected to sewage works, and development restricted in unsewered areas. The river board saw future problems because of the increasing use of agrochemicals, radioactive isotopes in industry and hospitals, and the volume of water used in large power stations. It also thought that 'the farmer, the broiler processor and others will have to accept more restrictions. Even the housewife may have to be restricted in her choice and use of synthetic detergents in the interests of clean rivers.'

The Tyne estuary was of particular importance, both economically, being the port of Newcastle, but also because the Tyne Corporation failed to stop other pollution and influenced local authorities responsible for pollution not to bring prosecutions. In 1927, 3,361 salmon were registered caught in the Tyne; by 1955 only three were caught. In 1959, the Tyne 'continued to fester on the densely populated borders of Northumberland and Durham' (ACA, 1959, 10, 1: 38). It was 'devastatingly foul' with 30 to 40 million gallons poured in every day to be swirled up and down the fourteen-mile estuary by the tide (ACA, 1959, 10, 1: 31).

A committee was established and commissioned a £5,000 (£61,470) study to look into pollution in the Tyne Estuary. In 1962, the chairman of the committee, Alderman Renwick, praised the work of seventeen riverside authorities that had co-operated in the clean-up effort and announced that proposed arrangements for sewage disposal should be ready by 1969. Costing between £10 and £12 million, the scheme involved constructing twin pipes along the banks of the river, discharging sewage beyond an undersea cliff. This may seem a modest success, but the committee was not certain that government would bear even some of the cost.

Unlawful maintenance?

John Eastwood understood well that financial maintenance of actions by third parties with no direct interest in a case is generally unlawful (Carty & Payne, 1998). For this reason, only ACA members could be assisted, and only cases that were of interest to other anglers were taken up. It was always made known to defendants when the ACA gave indemnities to plaintiffs. In *Martell and Others v. Consett Iron Co. Ltd* (1955, Ch. 165 EG 320; Court of Appeal, 1955, 1 All ER 481) the fundamental question was raised as to whether this common cause was a sufficient common interest in the eyes of the law to justify anglers generally in financing legal action by one particular angler or riparian owner to protect one particular piece of water.

This case struck at the heart of the ACA's activities. Consett Iron Company Limited claimed that the financial and technical assistance given by the ACA to its members amounted to illegal maintenance and was a criminal offence; that is, that the ACA had no proprietary interests in the action and therefore should not be allowed to fund it. Obviously, if this claim had been upheld it would have put an end to most of the ACA's legal activity.

Mr Justice Danckwerts considered the legal challenge in a hearing before the case proper could be heard. Consett's claim was rejected, the judge holding that anglers and others were justified and entitled to band together to protect rivers from pollution.

On appeal, Lord Justice Jenkins upheld the ruling, and held

that the range of relevant interests which was sufficient to justify the assistance given by the ACA was much wider than those claimed by the defendant. He said that maintenance could be extended to visitors and those who came to fish merely by permission of the owner, and that fishing-tackle dealers and proprietors of local hotels that relied on the anglers for business could maintain the action. Indeed, on the principle of mutual protection, those with interests in any river that might suffer the same fate could qualify. Within a year the ACA ensured that contributions to its fighting fund were made only by those who fell under Lord Jenkins's specification of 'common cause'.

> The legality of the ACA and its procedure have been challenged in the courts and upheld by the High Court and the Court of Appeal. Although we have always been prepared for such a challenge it would be idle to pretend that it did not cause some very anxious moments when it came, but by and large it was worth it as it procured for us invaluable guidance as to how and to what extent we may legally help our members. (*ACA Pollution Handbook*, fourth edition, 1957)

Maintaining good relations with polluters

The ACA has always taken the view that polluters are thoughtless rather than wilful and that, once they realise the harm they are doing, they are usually ready to negotiate. A new step for the ACA was taken along these lines with a paper mill proprietor in the case of *Wilmot v. Portals, John Allen and Sons Ltd* in 1964. The defendants admitted polluting and killing fish on the River Erme, and were ordered to pay damages to the plaintiff. However, they also submitted to a 'judgment by consent', which gave the plaintiffs liberty to apply for an injunction if pollution did not cease within three years (by 31 January 1967). In essence it gave the defendant one last chance, as a new pollution incident would result in an injunction, rather than contempt proceedings.

However, the plaintiffs were impressed by the defendants' willingness to co-operate, especially since the Erme had been polluted for over a century and the local authority had never attempted to halt pollution. Indeed, following this case the ACA submitted a complaint against the Ministry of Housing and Local Government about the apparent lack of concern on the part of local authorities about pollution damage. It stated that 'before anything can be done thousands of man hours and tens of thousands of pounds must be wasted on conferences and consultation with everybody who can have a conceivable interest in obstructing the effort of the river board[s] to clean up the disgusting state of the waters' (ACA, 1964, 15, 3: 35).

In general, relations between the ACA and defendants remained cordial – after all, the ACA never sought to punish anybody but simply to maintain healthy fisheries on behalf of members. An editorial in the *ACA Review* in 1957 had pointed out a difference in attitudes between commercial and public-sector defendants:

> We continue to find an increasing readiness on the part of industrial concerns to take voluntary action to remedy pollution. Local authorities, however, are still being difficult. No doubt some of them genuinely want to bring their sewage works up to date and to fulfil their statutory obligations under the Public Health Act and are only prevented from doing so by the refusal of the Ministry of Health to sanction the necessary work, but there are still a good many local authorities who simply have no intention

of spending money on avoiding pollution unless they are absolutely compelled to do so. In dealing with these local authorities we have to bear in mind that national considerations must prevail and to try to achieve a result which will remedy the injustice to the individual without upsetting the national economy.

The ACA became expert in ways of stopping and preventing pollution, and although it has no obligation it has always been very willing to give advice to polluters, both to save them from the expense of court action and to minimise the costs of technical improvements. The 1950 *ACA Review* reported that the ACA had anticipated a risk of pollution from a new housing estate in Berkshire and had drawn attention to it. The Newbury Rural District Council was proposing to build a surface-water sewer from the new estate into a small brook which flows into the River Lambourn. Although the local authority had statutory power to lay the sewer, the ACA thought it wise to point out that the effluent must satisfy the rights of riparian owners to an absolutely clean river, and not merely public health requirements.

A similar negotiation took place in the case of *Dent and Dent v. Harrogate Corporation* in 1962. Life in the River Crimple below the Harrogate sewage works' outfall was extinguished owing to effluent from the sewage works, which at times reduced the whole of the water in the stream to the quality of a substandard sewage effluent. Enquiries disclosed that Harrogate Corporation was aware of the position and had already prepared plans to modernise the sewage works. However, it also planned to increase capacity, which meant that the volume of effluent would be double the natural flow of the stream. This, the ACA were advised, was bound to cause pollution.

At that stage the Corporation could not, or would not, say what the quality of the effluent would be. 'In previous cases, local authorities against whom injunctions have been granted after they have built new sewage works have complained bitterly that it is much more expensive to make alterations and improvements after the works have been built than it would have been to do the job properly in the first instance, so this action was started in the hope of avoiding a similar situation' (ACA, 1962, 13, 4: 18-19).

The plaintiffs (Mr G. Dent and Mr J. H. Dent) asked for damages only for the existing pollution, and an injunction restraining the defendants from constructing or enlarging the sewage works without ensuring that they would cease to pollute the river.

Long after the writ was issued, the defendants stated that they intended to supplement the conventional treatment of the sewage with tertiary treatment by irrigation over grass roots. The plaintiffs were advised that, because of the lack of dilution, the defendants' actions would simply create another form of pollution from nitrate, phosphate and potash (the end products of 1960s sewage purification techniques), which, if present in excess, would cause uncontrollable growths of flannel weed, rushes and similar undesirable weed. The ACA also departed from normal practice by pointing out to the defendants that they could discharge the effluent from the new works into the River Nidd, where there was ample dilution for it, instead of into the Crimple. However, the defendants were not prepared to do this and maintained that the discharge of the effluent into the Crimple would not cause as much damage as was claimed by the plaintiffs.

The defendants agreed that the river had been clear previously, and had supported a good mixed fishery with coarse fish and trout. They agreed to pay full costs and restock, after their works were complete. Still, the Corporation decided to carry on with its plans and hope for the best. However, it was warned by the judge that it must not pollute by making sure that its releases had adequate dilution, and agreed that, should this occur, it would build a pipeline to discharge elsewhere, probably in the River Nidd. This was allowed by Mr Justice Plowman on 4 March 1962.

Pollution ceased after this incident with no repeat cases. This is a good example of how the ACA tried to negotiate a settlement to save taxpayers' money by making sure that sewage works were adequate. In other cases, there was no option but to spend considerable amounts of its own time and money to prevent determined local authorities from continuing to pollute.

Defences

Pollution is simply another aspect of the ancient laws of trespass and nuisance, which are part of the common law. It is an infringement of the owner's right to enjoy the use of his property without interference. These rights also apply to abstraction, as was established in *Edinburgh Water Trustees v. Sommerville & Son* (1906, 95 L.T. 217).[1] 'When an Act of Parliament authorises interference with the natural flow, the original rights of the riparian proprietors are impaired only so far as the reasonable exercise of the statutory rights impairs them' (Wisdom, 1979: 87).

There are two key defences to a common law action which affect river pollution. These are prescription and conduct permitted by statute.

---

1   See also *Medway Co. v. Romney (Earl)*, 1861, 4 L.T. 87.

Prescription

Pollution by custom, or plaintiffs granting pollution rights, is unusual. A prescriptive right is deemed to exist when a nuisance caused by the defendant has been continuing for a long period to the full knowledge of the plaintiff without complaint from the plaintiff (see *Sturges v. Bridgman*, 1879, 11 Ch. D. 852, 865).

A defendant who can show a prescriptive right has a good defence in an action for pollution. For example, he might show that he has been causing pollution for a long time (usually twenty years) and, as nobody has complained before, he has effectively attained the right. For example, a case of tin miners using a natural stream for washing ore was held to be 'good custom' since it was a reasonable use and limited to the necessary working of the mine (*Carlyon v. Lovering*, 1857, 1 H. & N. 784). However, as realised in *Goodman v. Saltash Corporation* (1882, 48 L.T. 39), prescription can only be claimed for something that has a lawful origin in common law. The discharge of untreated sewage into tidal waters polluting oyster beds (*Foster v. Warblington UDC*, 1906, 1 K.B. 648) was unacceptable and did not constitute an easement. Most important, if the defendant has secretly enjoyed the alleged easement to pollute and the plaintiff was unaware that pollution was occurring, then a prescriptive right is not granted (*Liverpool Corporation v. Coghill*, 1918, 1 CH. 307).

Prescription was the defence used in *Golden Hill Fishing Club v. Wansford Trout Farm* in 1986 in the ACA's first action against a trout farm. In 1982 the trout farm was polluting the West Beck, one of the best chalk streams in Britain. It was also abstracting large quantities of water which at times cut off all instream flows to the Beck.

The fish farm claimed the right to abstract and pollute by easement because it had been farming trout since 1955. The ACA challenged the defence by claiming that the level of abstraction and pollution had increased over time. As evidence they cited the sales revenue for the Wansford Trout Farm, which was £58,907 in 1973 but by 1981 had increased to £616,329 (roughly £200,000 in 1973 prices). Negotiations broke down and action in the High Court followed. The ACA's costs, had they lost, would have been in excess of £80,000 (£143,838). Nevertheless, when the ACA's Pollution Subcommittee met in London, it unanimously voted to go to the High Court.

In front of the judge, the trout farm backed down and agreed to remedy the conditions and pay costs and damages to the Golden Hill Fishing Club of £32,500 (£54,778).

Five years later the trout farm again polluted the West Beck, causing harm to the rights of the Golden Hill Fishing Club. The pollution in 1990/91 was held to be contempt of court since the farm had an injunction against it following its pollution in 1986. Mr Justice Henry fined it £500 (£842) for each breach of covenant (fourteen breaches in total). The managing director of the trout farm did not have his property sequestered nor was he sent to jail 'because of the efforts the company was now making to counter the pollution' (ACA, 1991, 3: 1-2). It put into operation pumps which increased its costs by £46,500 (£78,375), and a biological filter which cost £50,000 (£84,274).

This was a notable legal victory by the ACA in overcoming the defence of prescription, but the other defence, statute, is by far the more important. It is also more difficult to overcome as it arises through parliamentary legislation.

Statutory authority – private acts

The case of *Nicholl v. Penybont Main Sewerage Board* has already been mentioned with regard to the plaintiff being upstream from the polluter. But another aspect of the case was that the plaintiff had also asked for a mandatory order compelling the defendants to demolish and remove the valve and outfall, as they existed solely to discharge unpurified sewage which, in any case, was illegal under the Public Health Act. However, six years later, in January 1958, the Penybont Main Sewerage Board deposited a Private Bill with Parliament which would allow it to carry on discharging sewage as before. It was stated quite openly in the subsequent proceedings before Parliament that the sole purpose of the Bill was to have the injunction rescinded.

The Board had applied to the Ministry of Housing and Local Government, which then had the responsibility for cleaning up rivers, to give its special authority to the Private Bill. The Ministry strongly approved of the move, citing the expense of altering the sewage arrangements and claiming that the relevant section of the Public Health Act 'could not be complied with by any inland sewage disposal scheme at all'. Very soon after this, the Minister of Housing and Local Government, Mr Henry Brooke, stated publicly: 'I would dearly like to become known as the Minister for Clean Rivers.'

Fortunately, the Parliamentary Agents retained by the ACA noticed the Bill and action was taken to amend the Penybont Main Sewerage Bill so that the common law rights of riparian owners on the Ogmore and Ewenni rivers remained. Riparian owners on the Colne river were not so lucky when they referred a case of pollution from a new sewage works. The Hertfordshire County Council had pre-empted the ACA by some years when it promoted a Private Act to protect the Colne Valley Sewage Board from action against any polluting activity in 1937. The Act provided that 'no riparian owner or other party injured by the discharge of effluent from the Works shall have any right of actions against the Board either for an injunction or damages'.

In this case, the only way forward was for the ACA to table its own Private Bill to amend that of the Sewage Board. In the event, the ACA action did prompt improvements to be made and the pollution was brought under control. Had the plaintiffs been standing alone they would not have known about the removal of their rights nor been in a position to do anything about it. The parliamentary action in the Penybont case cost £2,500 (£33,709) to carry through – a sum well beyond most individuals.

Interpretation of what is unintentionally allowed by conduct permitted by the state is varied, and hence may include pollution as a by-product of a necessary and approved activity. It is, therefore, the most frequent defence. Other statutory defences have failed, for example (as mentioned above in the case of the Derby Corporation and the British Electricity Authority) because the authority to pollute was assumed to come with the statutory duty to perform public services, rather than expressly permitted.

5 HOW THE ACA AFFECTED GOVERNMENT POLICY AND LEGISLATION

River boards

River boards were created almost concurrently with the ACA itself under the River Boards Act of 1948. They replaced the struggling Fishery Boards and were charged with administering the Salmon and Freshwater Fisheries Acts and with land drainage, as well as with pollution prevention. As has been discussed above, the boards sometimes worked with the ACA, sometimes against them.

Despite good intentions, the government's river boards were never a success and brought very few actions against polluters. The Rivers (Prevention of Pollution) Act of 1951 made it an offence to discharge into any stream any poisonous, noxious or polluting matter, but the requirement remained that the consent of the Minister of Housing and Local Government was needed to prosecute local authorities for sewage pollution (Carty & Payne, 1998: 37). Since this same minister was busily authorising new housing programmes and was also responsible for providing loans to improve and renew sewage works, this presented obvious difficulties. The conflict was the basis of the poor management behind *Astor v. Sevenoaks RDC* referred to above (pp. 55–6).

Part of the problem was the background of decision-making committees, whose members had an interest in the water environment, but mainly from a commercial angle. Most were from local business, such as farmers and industrialists, or local government. Few, if any, were from fisheries, although some may have been landowners. Therefore, many of the members of the river boards were themselves potential polluters, and it is not surprising that the boards were unsuccessful in preventing pollution. A publication of the Federation (now Confederation) of British Industry around 1955 asked whether it was in the national interest that industry should be put to the expense of purifying its effluents for the sake of saving rivers in which the fishing rights were only worth a few pounds a year. But then it went on to say that where an industrialist wanted clean water for his processing, he would assert the same right that anglers were trying to uphold.

It became obvious where the allegiances of river board members lay from their influence on initial drafting of the Rivers (Prevention of Pollution) Act of 1951. Subsections 4 and 5 of Clause 4 were adopted with river board approval. In essence, these subsections stated that, provided a polluter kept to uniform emission standards set by the river boards, the polluter was not only safe from criminal prosecution but from civil action as well. This suggests a direct response to ACA actions brought in the common law (Bate, 2000).

Uniform emission standards

Uniform emission standards (UES) were proposed under the Rivers (Prevention of Pollution) Act, 1951, and applied to the quantity and quality of the effluent emitted. When originally suggested by the Royal Commission of 1912, the standards took notice of the impact that effluent would have on the receiving environment. In other words, it was not simply the amount or type of effluent which mattered, but also the size and flow of the river. However, in practice the assimilative capacity of the receiving environment was ignored, and the operation of UES omitted half the equation. It provided certainty for the polluter, but would lead to pollution. Fortunately, UES were never given statutory authority. They were interpreted as guidelines, allowing common law actions to proceed.

The river boards were also responsible for issuing abstraction licences, and it became clear that too many licences were being issued, causing serious depletion of instream flow and exacerbating the problems of UES. Being unable to alter the terms of a licence for two years, the river boards demanded more powers to deal with the very problems they themselves had created (ACA, 1960, 11, 4: 60).

Because of business lobbying aimed at ensuring that UES should protect polluters, the ACA maintained a running campaign against such statutory protection. It spent considerable sums reminding government officials that UES, if defined as a statutory authorisation by government, would stop any common law action against a polluter complying with their UES, regardless of the pollution caused (Bate, 2000).

Acknowledging the power of the interests against it and in favour of UES, the ACA suggested a compromise to the government. The common law should remain as it was (hence UES were not statutory authorisations and would not undermine the common law) but, in any case where national economic interests might have been affected by any common law action, the Attorney-General could apply to the court for an extension of time before the order of the court (such as an injunction) became operative. This amendment was supported by members on both sides of the House (including the chair of the relevant standing committee, Enoch Powell, MP for Wolverhampton West), and in the end the minister withdrew the two subsections that would have undermined common law. This was the first instance in which the ACA successfully influenced public policy, largely through thousands of ACA members writing letters to their MPs (Bate, 2000).

Despite creating new pollution offences, the Act set down such onerous restrictions on collection and presentation of evidence that river boards were seriously handicapped in proving offences. Gerrish, the ACA's solicitor, wrote in an editorial on the common law in 1957: 'We believe that not a single polluter has been prosecuted under the Act since it was passed in 1951.' On the other hand, despite being a 'band of amateurs . . . that cannot afford to employ whole time Pollution Officers, Fishery Officers or to set up and staff technical laboratories . . . we think that, by assisting our members to apply common law, the ACA has achieved more in the last six years to reduce river pollution and estuarial pollution than all the River Boards put together.'

Committee on Salmon and Freshwater Fisheries, 1960

This committee, chaired by Lord Bledisloe, analysed existing legislation as it affected freshwater fisheries. Under pressure from commercial interests to relax their duty of care, the committee stated unanimously that no alteration should be made to the common law. It also made one other significant recommendation – to delete the word 'knowingly' from Section 8 of the Salmon and Freshwater Fisheries Act of 1923. The 'knowingly' clause had meant that prosecutions under the Act could only succeed where a duty of care on the part of the defendant had been breached. Pollution causing fish kill was not enough; the defendant had knowingly to cause that pollution – an accident did not count for success in a prosecution (Carty & Payne, 1998: 36). In principle this deletion strengthened the powers of the river boards, as strict liability is easier to prove than a breach of duty (ACA, 1961, 12, 3: 45), but it made little change in practice. The ACA had advised the committee and supported several of the recommendations, such as the removal of the ministerial power to veto prosecutions under the 1951 Act, but was disappointed that the river boards still had to collect effluent samples in triplicate if they were to be used as evidence in any legal proceedings. Neither did the ACA agree with the committee's interpretation of the penal legislation regarding multiple pollution – that there can be no conviction without specific proof against every defendant.

Rivers (Prevention of Pollution) Act, 1961

This Act brought into existence many of the recommendations of the Trade Effluents Subcommittee of the Central Water Authority Committee (1960), usually referred to as the Armer Committee, after its chairman. This period marks the lowest point of relations between government and the ACA. The influence and success of the ACA were becoming a threat to nationalised interests, which were of paramount importance to the government of the day.

The largest representation for change in the common law came from sections of the Federation (now Confederation) of British Industry, mainly the British Iron and Steel Federation. The Gas Council and the National Coal Board also supported the proposed changes. In their deposition, the Federation of British Industry cited the ACA's first case (*Lord Brocket v. Luton Corporation*, 1946, pp. 27–9 above), saying that generally the business community could not comply with injunctions, and hence the common law should not be allowed to work. In the Brocket case the designers of the sewage works said that they could not comply with the Royal Commission standards (Bate, 1994). Since Lord Brocket had no fishery and was satisfied with the amelioration in pollution he did not enforce his rights, so the analogy is a false one.

The ACA was invited to give evidence before the Armer Committee. Although its advice was heeded, the committee still recommended that the rights of riparian owners and anglers should be attenuated if it could be shown 'that the operation of the common law was unduly onerous, or had led to the closing of industrial works, or had raised the cost of production' (cited in Bate, 2000: 100). This seems to indicate that the committee was not aware of the importance of external costs (pollution) from the production process. However, it is more likely that the committee was responding to special interests – polluting businesses and communities that did not want to bear the full costs of enforced property rights. In short, the Armer Committee was saying that business should not have to pay for its pollution and the common law should be changed accordingly. The committee noted that the 'common law remedy had been invoked more frequently in recent years under the influence of the ACA . . . and that some pressure had been put on polluters in consequence' (cited in ACA, 1960, 11, 1: 2).

The Act recognised the impossibility of setting uniform emission standards and substituted a system of licensing each effluent according to its merits. This was still not satisfactory as licences could not be varied for two years. This meant that where licences were already operating at the maximum, no new industry could be given a licence without causing pollution. In practice, either the new industry was banned until the current licences ran out and tighter ones could be issued, or a new discharge licence must be issued regardless of pollution.

To make matters worse, the Rivers (Prevention of Pollution) Act, 1961 (Section 12), disallowed the use of fish toxicity tests in river board prosecutions, which compounded the difficulties of collecting samples to qualify as evidence. This change prevented prosecution as long as the emitter was meeting set standards, even if the river was grossly polluted.

The Water Resources Act, 1963

When this Act was at committee stage, sponsored by the Minister for Housing and Local Government, proposals were heard which would have undermined the power of the common law to combat excess abstraction. 'Abstraction of water from streams on the surface or from underground sources should be subject to a licence [which confers] a statutory right to reduce the flow of the river . . . and should override all common law rights of riparian owners or anglers' (ACA, 1962, 13, 2: 17, citing the subcommittee on water resources). This proposal made common law action against abstractors even more difficult. It was also inequitable. For example, if an abstractor reduced the flow of a river, an emitter of effluent might inadvertently cause pollution, and be liable to prosecution while the abstractor went free. As the ACA put it, 'Abstraction . . . is the handmaiden of pollution' (ACA, 1973, 19, 4: 6).

The Act had three major stated aims:

- to improve conservation of water resources;
- to secure abstractors' rights by establishing new abstraction licences; and
- to set minimum acceptable instream flows.

The ACA was concerned that establishing new abstraction licences would probably lead to excess abstraction. Indeed, in his report on the 1963 Act for the ACA, Mr J. S. Barclay stated that it was clear that the government thought that riparian owners should be happy to give up their common law rights in exchange for the security of the minimum acceptable flow. Mr Barclay had been part of a deputation called 'The United Fishermen', which included several MPs and represented the ACA, the Salmon and Trout Association, the British Field Sports Association, the National Federation of Anglers and the National Council of Salmon Netsmen. The United Fishermen made their case to the Minister of Housing and Local Government. They argued that instream flows would be set only on major rivers, not small fishing rivers, and might take several years to implement.

Eventually, on third reading, a clause did appear which gave a special right of appeal for anglers against a new licence if the sport fishery owner could reasonably demonstrate that the fishery would be damaged by the abstraction (ACA, 1963, 14, 4: 48). Another amendment, arising from points made by fishermen, required that an abstractor would have to prove that he could comply with the licence, although ministerial approval could be sought by potential abstractors to allow abstraction regardless of cost. These small battles to retain civil rights were hard won. Even though no instream flows were ever set because the river authority officials were not given the resources to do it, it was necessary to fight (Bate, 1994).

In 1965, river boards were superseded by River Authorities, which would have the power to assess what was an acceptable minimum 'instream' flow for each river. (It was apparent that the government was finally acknowledging the significance of dilution.) Because of the decision to set instream flow requirements, the ACA supported the new River Authorities (ACA, 1965, 16, 1).

But, yet again, the Ministry of Health adopted effluent standards that ignored the dilution factor. Over the next few years sewage increased rapidly with industrial development and the demands for domestic use, and the dilution factor became so low that pollution incidents led to increased ACA legal actions.

In 1968, a case was brought to the ACA regarding the River Medway in Kent. The local authority had refused consent for a building development because it would have aggravated the already serious pollution problems. The landowners appealed to the Minister of Housing and Local Government, and the ACA submitted a memorandum to the minister on behalf of anglers and fishery owners and in support of the local authority. If an alert local newspaper reporter had not warned the ACA and other interested parties – including the River Authority – the minister would have made the decision *in camera*, based on written statements, without public notice or giving anyone the opportunity to call evidence or cross-examine witnesses. The minister was persuaded to hold a public inquiry, but the handling of the case could have given little assurance about the attitude of the ministry, which was supposed to ensure the 'wholesomeness' of rivers.

An article on abstraction in the *Flyfishers' Journal* of winter 1969 pointed to several weaknesses of River Authorities and their governing body, the Water Resources Board, which was manned largely by engineers – freshwater biology and ecology were not well represented. The River Authorities, which assessed applications for abstraction licences, were also heavily weighted with engineers, but also comprised officials from the very water companies applying for more water. It also became clear during a public inquiry to save the River Stour, a chalk stream in Kent, that the water company engineer recommended sinking a borehole into the source of the river, as this was the cheapest method of abstraction. It would also mean the death of the river, since it was felt by many objectors, including the Kent Trust for Nature Conservancy, the Canterbury Society, the Canterbury and District Natural History Society, three fishing clubs and many riparian owners, that the proposed abstraction was grossly excessive for the size of the river. In this case, the Minister of Housing and Local Government effected a compromise and allowed the water company to double its abstraction rather than triple it.

The Water Act, 1973

This Act created new regional Water Authorities which had responsibility for both sewage disposal and pollution control. So the situation again arose of an authority prosecuting itself for pollution.

The Water Authorities were charged with bringing sewage works up to standard, but it soon became clear that they had insufficient funds to do the job. The *ACA Review* of winter 1974 described the gargantuan task before the new Authorities:

> They have inherited hundreds of inadequate, out-of-date
> sewage plants. A glance at the last-published reports of the
> old River Authorities shows a measure of their task: *Devon*:
> Number of samples of effluents 919. Unsatisfactory 498.

> *Great Ouse*: Number of river samples 4,151. Doubtful 872.
> Unsatisfactory 707. *Lancashire*: Number of samples of
> effluents 769. 43.7 per cent failed to meet the 'Royal
> Commission' standard. *Lea Conservancy*: Number of samples
> of effluents 728. Unsatisfactory 210. *Severn*: Number of
> samples of sewage effluents 976. Unsatisfactory 306.

Within a year of the Water Authorities' formation, the Conservative government had drastically reduced their budgets. The following Labour government introduced economy measures that caused the anti-pollution measures of the accompanying Control of Pollution Act to be scaled back. The Authorities were reduced to relying entirely on water rates levied on users – rates that did not reflect the cost of supply.

The Severn-Trent Regional Water Authority set up an independent Water Quality Advisory Panel which surveyed the new region and reported in 1975. The panel found that about 22 per cent of the effluent discharged into the watercourses in the area was unsatisfactory. The chairman of the panel, Mr Edward Franklin, stated: 'It is sad to record that governments over the years have found it easier to pass Acts of Parliament than to find the funds to implement them.'

It was originally envisaged and promised that the new Water Authorities would impose satisfactory standards on industrial effluents, but within two years this seemed a remote possibility as the Authorities could do so little to achieve comparably high standards in their own sewage works.

The *ACA Review* of 1975 concluded that: 'Anyone who believes that statutory measures can clear up pollution should think again: there is no substitute for the common law.'

Control of Pollution Act (COPA), 1974

COPA supplemented the Water Act of 1973 and during its long reading stage was known as the Protection of the Environment Bill. As with the Water Act, its original scope proved over-ambitious. The build-up to this Act highlights the powerful political position that anglers, and the ACA in particular, were creating for themselves. From the nadir of the Armer Committee, the ACA was now enjoying very good relations with government.

The government published its fifth consultation paper in 1971 in which it proposed to abolish the common law rights in respect of pollution caused by discharges that a Water Authority had authorised. The only remedy available would be compensation for damage caused – an injunction would no longer be available – effectively creating a licence to pollute.

The ACA's Chairman, Dermot Wilson, launched a campaign against the proposals. 'Our sister organisations – the National Anglers' Council, the National Federation of Anglers and the Salmon and Trout Association – all used their considerable influence.' They supported Lord Bledisloe and Viscount Dilhorne, who spoke in the House of Lords against the proposals, and the government was persuaded to withdraw the relevant clause of the Bill.

The ACA even boasted that 'we have helpful contacts at both government and parliamentary level' (ACA, 1976, 22, 1: 3). In 1972, the ACA was called in for negotiations with Mr Eldon Griffiths, the Under-Secretary of State for the Environment. According to an ACA editorial, this call came because of substantial pressure from the ACA members who had written to their MPs demanding changes in government policies towards anglers.

In November 1972, Mr Griffiths announced in Parliament: 'I have met the Anglers' Co-operative Association. As a result we have been able to accept some suggestions for revision of the proposals relating to common law rights' (ACA, 1972, 19, 2: 6). Because of ACA persistence, Mr Griffiths agreed that rights to bring common law actions for damages against all dischargers of effluents would remain absolutely as they stood, '*whether or not* the discharger in question had complied with a water authority's "consent"' (ACA, 1972, 19, 2: 6, emphasis in original). 'This is the most important single concession we could have gained and – let there be no mistake about it – it represents a truly notable achievement . . . One further aspect of this decision is that industry will continue to find the money for all such damages, whereas it was originally proposed that the taxpayer should do so in certain circumstances' (ACA, 1972, 19, 2: 6).

The minority of the ACA wishes that were not accepted related to injunctions. Crucially, it was suggested that 'In order that industrialists should be freed from the risk of having to shut down factories overnight, perhaps without due cause, the Government has decided that they should be exempted from injunctions if – *and only if* – they have complied faithfully with the conditions of a water authority's consent' (ACA, 1972, 19, 2: 6, emphasis in original).

The ACA contested this clause, even though it thought it would be unnecessary to ask for an injunction in a case where a polluter had complied with his discharge permit. It argued that it would be theoretically possible for a factory owner to 'purchase' a licence to pollute – simply by continuing to pay damages over an extended period of time, in lieu of cleaning up his discharge. 'But we have sought and received a reassurance from the Government that legislation will make this impossible' (ACA, 1972, 19, 2: 8). It appeared, after all, that the ACA might not fight this change, which may have been because of the extremely good relations at the time between the ACA and the Under-Secretary.

An ACA editorial even quoted Eldon Griffiths complimenting the ACA on its past conduct: 'I am sure that most people with concern for the environment will recognise that common law actions have been one of the main defences – and sometimes the only defence – against river pollution; and that even with our proposed improvements in administration and control we could ill afford to do without them' (ACA, 1972, 19, 2: 21).

Broadening of legal standing

A significant change was proposed for COPA. The Act would enable any member of the public to bring an action against any emitter of pollutants, including Water Authorities, whose effluent discharge did not comply with the laid-down consent conditions. Prior to this Act, only the government authority had been able to prosecute a polluter. Under the common law, one had needed a proprietary interest in the water harmed to bring an action. This new venture would mean that, in principle, an activist in Scotland could prosecute a polluter in Cornwall.

Although a 'paper' victory in the battle to keep injunctions had been won under COPA, it by no means followed that water quality would improve or even remain the same as before. On 5 August 1975, the UK Department of the Environment announced that implementation of Part II of the Control of Pollution Act was to be postponed indefinitely. As all the more effective statutory measures to contain or reduce pollution were included in Part II, such as the broadening of legal standing, this was a major setback.

The ACA was even more dismayed when, in the following year,

the government announced an easing of emission standards. It would have been politically embarrassing to introduce COPA Part II when about 30 per cent of discharges to rivers did not comply with the existing legal standards. According to ACA, the 'consent conditions are being revised, just to make sure that there aren't any embarrassing legal actions' (ACA, 1978: 3). It is likely that this measure was intended to ensure that Part II of COPA 1974 could be brought into effect. The ACA editorial was very scornful of this move: 'You don't make the effluents comply with the standards. You make the standards comply with the effluents. It's as simple as that' (ibid).

Meanwhile the normal operations of the ACA were continuing at maximum capacity. Several new Water Authorities immediately became involved in cases on the Rivers Amman and Loughor in South Wales, the Horse Eye sewer in Sussex, the River Tern in Shropshire, the River Teise in Kent, and the Rivers Thames and Ray in Wiltshire – this last with claims totalling £46,489 (£223,795). The solicitors were dealing with more cases than ever before, although the ACA made it clear that this was more an effect of growing awareness of the ACA and a general concern for the environment than that rivers were getting dirtier. The *ACA Review* reported an improvement as early as 1951. Pollution on the River Colne in 1964 ceased immediately after the publication of a *Review* in which the case had been mentioned.

The ACA also suffered from the deep economic recession that had prompted the budgetary cutbacks to COPA and the Water Authorities. Printing and postal rates soared, and the ACA Committee decided to restrict the issue of the *Review* to one a year – a change which remains in force today. These changes were made so that members' interests could be protected as before.

A case in early 1975 must have prompted a few wry smiles in the ACA office when investigations into a pollution incident almost descended into farce. A road tanker had overturned, causing pollution and fish kill in the River Rother in Sussex. The ACA experts were planning an electro-fishing investigation when another tanker owned by the same firm overturned in the same place, causing further pollution. This case was quickly settled, and by the next issue £4,313 (£20,763) had been recovered in damages.

Despite setbacks, conditions were improving, and the ACA was encouraged when the appropriately named Mr Hugh Fish, the newly appointed Chief Executive of the Thames Water Authority, reported in 1978 that cleaning rivers was a good investment. He told a meeting of the Institute of Municipal Engineers that the £100 million that had been spent on cleaning up the River Thames since the early 1960s had more than paid for itself, not merely in environmental benefit but in supplying fresh water. During the drought of 1976 the river had given an extra 150 million gallons a day to guarantee supply.

Not so encouraging was the statement made by the Rt Hon. Michael Heseltine, PC, before he took up his post as Secretary of State for the Environment in 1979: 'Progress against pollution requires a healthy economy. You can hardly expect Environmental Health Officers to insist that standards at a local factory be improved when the consequences may be that production has to stop because the necessary improvements cannot be afforded.' In a subsequent debate in the House of Lords, Lord Beaumont of Whitley commented: 'I interpret that as saying that it's all right poisoning people if you are not making money at the same time.'

In a paper on the effect of pollution given to the Countryside Sports Conference in 1979, the ACA made the point that, a century after water pollution became a criminal offence, the government aimed to legalise thousands of polluting effluents. When the Royal Commission Standard was introduced in 1912, it was welcomed by local authorities and industrialists for giving them some latitude in disposing of their effluents. By the end of 1979, the Royal Commission Standard was considered too high for many of the effluent discharges and was abolished to make way for the implementation of the second part of COPA.

COPA Part II was still not fully implemented ten years after Part I, and the ACA concluded that 'when it is (if it is) factories that have been polluting Britain's rivers for decades will carry on polluting. They will either be exempt from the Act's controls, or they will have obtained what are known as "deemed consents". One of the main aims of the legislation was to enable members of the public to prosecute any firm or individual who failed to keep the consent conditions. There is little possibility of that happening for the simple reason that "consents" have been tailored to fit polluters' requirements. In short, the Act will legalise pollution' (ACA, 1984: 3).

The ACA Annual Report of 1981 declared that the fighting fund, now not used as frequently to fight common law actions as in the early days, had been rebuilt and was substantial enough to cover any eventuality. In 1983, damages recovered over the previous ten years had amounted to around £300,000 (at least £600,000) and, with the assurance of a healthy fighting fund, the ACA took on some more complex cases.

A new Water Act came into force in October 1983, the main provisions of which were to increase the Water Authorities' borrowing powers in an attempt to enable replacements of ancient sewage works; and the removal of the requirement to hold main

Authority and committee meetings in public. The agreement by the Authorities' chairmen to keep the press and public informed through press conferences was viewed sceptically by the ACA.

In October 1983, 13,500 litres of flux oil leaked into the River Tees upstream of Darlington. It killed fish over a twenty-mile stretch of the river. The Northumbrian Water Authority (NWA) used water from Kielder Reservoir by operating tunnels that connect the Tyne, Wear and Tees to flush the oil away. Acting on behalf of the Tees Fisheries Action Committee, which represented 52 claimants, in *ACA Trustees Ltd v. Northumbrian Water Authority* (1983) the ACA negotiated two interim payments of £20,000 (£32,403) from the NWA, which was spent on restocking the river. In October 1987 a final settlement was obtained which lifted the total figure to a record £352,684 (£571,402; ACA, 1988: 10-11).

The Control of Pollution Act Part II, Section 32, was eventually passed in August 1985, and the ACA soon took the opportunity to test its efficacy. On 14 May 1987, the ACA mounted its 'first-ever statutory prosecution to highlight the fact that those charged with preventing pollution are often polluters themselves' (ACA, 1988: 10). In mid-May the magistrates at Aylesbury heard six specimen charges of pollution in *ACA Trustees Ltd v. Thames Water Authority*. The charges alleged that on 11 September 1986, and on five subsequent dates, the TWA caused sewage effluent to enter the River Thames, breaching the conditions of Consent No. 1365 of Section 32 (1) of the Control of Pollution Act, 1974 (COPA), Part II.

The Authority pleaded guilty to the charges and was fined £1,000 (£1,620) on each of the counts. In addition to this it was ordered to pay £800 (£1,296) costs. The ACA's successful prosecution of the Thames Water Authority was widely covered in the national press. The case also received enthusiastic approval from anglers, and led to further successful prosecutions, such as against the Anglian Water Authority in 1988.

Privatisation

In the discussion leading up to water privatisation in 1989, Environment Secretary John Patten wrote an article in the *ACA Review* to attempt to convince anglers that privatisation was essential. He said, 'in future, quality objectives for our rivers will be set on a statutory basis – by the Authorities themselves. There will be new powers to ensure that Authorities give effect to environmental policies – and a new government inspectorate to advise on their exercise of environmental functions and to check the quality of their own effluent discharge' (ACA, 1989: 11).

The ACA was unconvinced by Patten's statement, criticising previously unfulfilled government promises to clean up rivers and pass beneficial legislation. They were scathing about the eleven-year wait for the enforcement of COPA Part II – even then 'some parts of the Act have never been implemented' (ACA, 1989: 11) – and hostile to the government's plans. Despite considerable improvements in the quality of river water, there was still a sizable problem that would be left to private enterprise to clear up. More than two thousand miles of British rivers were polluted in 1988, and 2,700 sewage outfalls failed to comply with their consent conditions for discharge. Drinking-water supplies were affected by sewage in Cornwall, Bristol, Luton, Manchester, East Anglia, Oxford and parts of Scotland. Thirty per cent of bathing beaches were polluted and failed to meet EC standards.

The ACA thought that the National Rivers Authority (NRA), the new government inspectorate, was a step in the right direction.

However, it was concerned that the NRA, like the river boards, would be ineffectual. 'At present there is nothing [the NRA] can do, because in order to make a success of water privatisation the government gave legal permission to the water authorities to discharge sewage into rivers pending the building of adequate sewage works, so the NRA, like an army awaiting its supplies of ammunition, will only be able to tackle the problem when the Government's derogations expire in a few years' time' (ACA, 1990: 4).

Nevertheless, the ACA co-operated with the NRA in several actions. The NRA was to benefit from a change in public, and hence political, sympathy from producer to environmental and consumer interests. The resulting switch in emphasis was manifested in 'green' legislation, which partly sprang from the strong showing of the Green Party in the 1989 European elections and the collapse of the Berlin Wall in the same year. Leftist interests moved from overtly political to covertly 'green' agendas, which accompanied a groundswell of public concern over the environment (see Maxey, 1999, and Rabkin and Sheehan, 1999, for discussions). As a result, the NRA was given the power to deliver environmental protection, unlike its predecessors. The NRA fast developed a good reputation for combating pollution of English rivers, and continued to co-operate with the ACA until it became part of the Environment Agency in 1995.

The NRA was helped by the separation of the environmental protection function of the former Water Authorities from the provision of water and sewerage services. Furthermore, according to Carty (2000), a system of integrated pollution control (IPC) was introduced by the Environmental Protection Act, 1990, which was the first system of its type in Europe. IPC analyses the whole environment rather than one receiving media, which 'has benefited the environment', he concluded.

The NRA took action against several newly privatised water companies, but private individuals brought the first-ever action against a water company in *Leek and District Fly Fishing Club (Staffordshire Branch) v. Severn Trent Water* in 1992. The club alleged that it had suffered damage to its fishery from effluent from the Leekbrook sewage treatment works. Under an agreement between the two parties the plaintiffs did not demand an interim injunction, in 'exchange for a High Court order providing for a "speedy trial"', with a full hearing to take place not later than 20 July 1992. At that time delays in bringing a case to court were significant. As ACA Director Allen Edwards commented at the time: 'Although the July 20 deadline is almost 8 months ahead, it is still very much sooner than such proceedings would normally be heard' (ACA, 1992, 2: 15). In fact, the matter was settled between the plaintiff and defendant by an undisclosed amount before the case came up. Although this case tested the mechanism of the common law under new conditions, it proved to be a very ordinary case.

The ACA and the NRA

The clarity of riparian property rights and the greater experience of the ACA in fighting river pollution sometimes meant that, in the co-operation between the ACA and the NRA, it was the ACA which played the dominant role.

Bury St Edmunds Angling Association and the Anglian National Rivers Authority v. Clarke (1993) illustrates many elements in the process of pollution control, including inadequate statutory powers, bureaucratic incompetence and a recidivist polluter with doubtful financial standing, and is worth describing in detail.

The defendant, a farmer, was alleged to have polluted the Rivers Blackbourne and Little Ouse in Suffolk with pig slurry in 1988. The angling club referred the case to the ACA. Since the regional NRA was already pursuing a prosecution against the same man, to avoid duplication of effort further action had to wait until evidence and copy statements could be released after the criminal trial. However, preliminary negotiations revealed that, unlike most polluters the ACA deals with, the farmer was uninsured.

Anglian NRA decided to restock the river and claim against the farmer for its expenses under Section 115 of the Water Act, 1991. The ACA's solicitors advised vigorously against this as a 'club's common law claim is often much more convincing than a claim under Section 115'. As expected, the claim soon ran into trouble and the NRA instructed the ACA solicitors to act for it to recover damages for the restocking programme. The total claim of the club and the NRA was running at about £60,000 (£71,400) when the farmer made an offer of final settlement of £10,000 (£11,900).

Meanwhile, the farmer was fined £10,000 but won an appeal against this fine on a technicality. He then lodged a defence to the civil action both denying causing pollution and claiming that the pollution was caused by act of God. As the total claim increased to £70,000 (£83,300), the ACA solicitors learned that the defendant had already been prosecuted by the NRA six times, and that if he had paid to have the slurry properly removed by lorry rather than let it wash into the river, it would have cost him over £100,000 (£119,000).

The case was then held up for exactly one year because the NRA failed to hand its file on the case over to the ACA. Some desultory negotiation took place and a trial date was set, but then postponed while the defendant had major back surgery. Prospects of recovering damages for the angling club and the NRA's costs of restocking receded as enquiry agents tried in vain to establish the extent of the defendant's assets. The defendant announced that he was acting for himself in the case, having fallen out with his solicitor over payment of an interim bill. Nevertheless, the NRA wanted to pursue the case to trial and agreed to meet two-thirds of the costs.

As the trial date approached, the ACA undertook negotiations to try to reduce the estimated ten-day hearing by agreeing some of the least controversial claims. The defendant, who was taking advice from a fishery expert, was co-operative, and a settlement began to look more likely.

On the morning of the trial, 9 July 1993, the defendant admitted liability, but the trial still continued for two weeks over the issue of the amount of damages. Judgment was finally obtained for the club at £8,480 (£9,703) for loss of amenity based on subscription income plus 50 per cent; and for the NRA at £50,000, although there was some confusion over this amount. While costs were being decided, the club's damages were paid – following a visit from the sheriffs. Eventually, in February 1994, nearly six years after the offence, the defendant was ordered to pay £52,500 (£59,850) in costs and £47,000 (£53,580) to the NRA. He made a one-off payment of £52,500 and agreed to pay off the balance in weekly instalments of £1,000 (£1,140).

Just before the trial, the ACA solicitors learned that the defendant had paid his fishery advisers by return of post and had recently made a very large investment in updated piggery equipment. Removing the pig slurry would have cost the same either way for the farmer, at least in nominal terms, but permitting the pollution had allowed him seven years in total before full payment was made. Since he was seemingly financially secure at the time of the trial and able to manage payments, the defendant must have been satisfied with the process. The club's losses were not severe, but the outcome was satisfactory in that pollution that had recurred over many years was finally stopped. The NRA emerges with least credit. Its sixth prosecution against the defendant failed after two court hearings – creating expense for the taxpayer. The effects of its decision to restock against advice were compounded by its incompetence in providing documentation and caused extra work and delay for the ACA solicitors. Although costs were largely met by the polluter, it is likely that they would have been lower and the matter resolved much more quickly had the NRA not been involved at all.

Minewater test case

In 1992, the ACA took on the very risky and seemingly insuperable problem of pollution caused by flooded, decommissioned coal mines. *ACA Trustees Ltd v. British Coal* (1992) was the case that generated the most publicity for the ACA since the Pride of Derby. It prosecuted British Coal over pollution of the River Rhymney in South Wales, alleging that contaminated water from a closed-down colliery had caused pollution and killed fish. The nationalised coal industry had been protected by statute and no common law actions had hitherto been possible. The summons issued under the Water Resources Act, 1991, which made the offence a criminal rather than a civil matter, claimed 'that the discharge was caused by the cessation of pumping at Britannia colliery, which stopped mining operations in 1990'. The outcome of the case depended on whether British Coal 'knowingly permitted' pollution to reach the river. Until that time, switching off the pumps at a disused pit had not fulfilled this condition (ACA, 1993, 2: 4). A successful prosecution would impose an enormous burden on British Coal – a declining industry – as it would have to continue to pump out numerous pits recently abandoned as uneconomical.

The judge at Cardiff Crown Court ruled that there was insufficient evidence to show that British Coal had 'knowingly polluted' the Rhymney, and hence the ACA lost only its third case ever. However, the judge said that the costs of £120,000 (£143,314) should be paid from government funds because of the importance of the ACA's action. The ACA appealed because, as one of its legal advisers concluded, 'contrary to this ruling, the ferruginous discharge into the Rhymney was foreseeable' (ACA, 1994, 2: 3).

The significance of this case extended far beyond the River Rhymney. Perhaps as many as 450 miles of rivers in England and Wales are affected by discharges from abandoned mines. Potentially the most dramatic example is the River Wear in Co. Durham. The river and its tributaries are home to migratory salmon and sea trout, but with the closure of the area's last big colliery (Easington) several years ago, there are growing fears that the eventual termination of pumping could result in the rivers becoming almost totally lifeless.

The National Rivers Authority signed a formal agreement with British Coal whereby it will receive at least fourteen days' notice of any intention to suspend pumping, and the ACA solicitor, Simon Jackson, sought the same consideration. If necessary, the NRA (now the Environment Agency) could then seek legal action to prevent pollution occurring, rather than bringing a prosecution after the damage had occurred.

The 1995 Coal Industry Act created the Coal Authority and

transferred to it ownership of all coal mines. While ownership of coal seams in the Britannia colliery was the subject of a preliminary hearing, the Authority continued pumping and undertook to keep angling interests informed of developments in terms of dealing with the problem.

April 1995 saw the formation of the Environment Agency, which was to co-ordinate the system of integrated pollution control and provide an 'environment one stop shop', regulating water, land and air pollution under one roof.

The litigation over the River Rhymney was compromised in 1996 by an agreement to set up a task group charged with commissioning a study and ultimately finding a solution to the problem. The River Rhymney Task Group comprised the Environment Agency, the Coal Authority, the Welsh Office, the Caerphilly County Borough Council and angling clubs, and was chaired by the ACA. The Task Group produced an environmental report in 1999 suggesting methods of remedying the problem, and economic consultants prepared a cost–benefit study of the various options. These are still under review at the time of writing.

Recent and proposed legislation

The European Council Directive 96/61/EC saw the introduction of the Pollution Prevention and Control Act, 1999, bringing more processes under the integrated pollution control regime. Carty (2000) considers that this has already improved the riverine environment.

In one respect the ACA was correct to be concerned about the legislation that followed privatisation. Section 48 (2) of the Water Resources Act (1991) gave a defence to a common law action if the conditions of an abstraction licence had been properly fulfilled (Carty & Payne, 1998). The ACA has lobbied against this section ever since, but to May 2001 with no success.

The water abstraction regime is currently under review by the Environment Agency. New proposals include the introduction of time-limited licences, the restitution of common law rights to relief from harm caused by over-abstraction, the abolition of licences of right, and the revocation of licences causing environmental harm. In addition a consultation process on fisheries legislation is continuing, with reports due to be published in 2001. The recommendations are likely to include new fishery plans, a new environmental court to deal with pollution (it is hoped this will make the ACA's job easier), and making siltation of rivers an environmental offence.

In search of genetic purity

There is no doubt that the Environment Agency has had a beneficial impact on the environment and has pursued polluters, often bringing thousands of prosecutions a year (see Carty & Payne, 1998). The ACA works closely and harmoniously with the Agency, and exchanges of evidence and advice are made in both directions. However, sometimes the Agency itself is the cause of problems such as over-abstraction or repair works, and it also shows a worrying tendency towards bureaucratic excess.

In 1997, the Environment Agency damaged fishing on the River Stour in Suffolk through over-abstraction, and more recently caused further problems through rebuilding the Pitmire weir on the same river. In carrying out these works, the Agency ruined the barbel fishing on a stretch leased by a syndicate. When the syndicate applied to the Agency to replace the fish, the Agency objected on the ground that barbel are not indigenous to the river – indeed, the syndicate stocked the river itself with the barbel in the early nineties. The ACA is currently in negotiation with the Agency over its restocking policy.

A similar dispute has arisen over restocking the River Frome in Dorset, which is a chalk stream normally offering excellent trout fishing. As with many rivers in Britain, a combination of over-abstraction, drought and overfishing has led to a dearth of trout in the river. In an attempt to restock it, local landowners proposed to introduce farmed brown trout from the nearby Hook river. These plans were opposed by an officer of the Environment Agency because of his concern about genetic pollution.

Although there are genetic differences between the trout on the various rivers, these differences are tiny. There is absolutely no evidence that any serious harm to the genetic stock will occur from restocking, but the Agency is prohibiting it, hiding behind the 'precautionary principle'. It is prohibiting action not because of a known harm but because of a theoretical one (see Morris, 2000, for a discussion of the problems inherent in the use of the precautionary principle). This 'principle' would enable the Agency to interfere with or even stop many lawful activities of fishery owners. Without restocking, the value of the fishery will remain low, and fewer fishermen will have a direct interest in the quality of the water or be available to monitor pollution. If the precautionary principle becomes established, the powers of the Environment Agency will be so extensive that local landowners and fishermen, who are responsible for the river being in such good condition, will be denied the opportunity to develop and maintain the riverine environment (Slocock, 2000).

The planning powers of the Environment Agency and other bodies, such as the Department of Environment, Transport and the Regions, are discussed at some length by Carty and Payne (1998: 215–233). There are numerous other Acts that interfere with landowners' rights (see Pennington, 1997, for a discussion and references).

6 CONCLUSION

English common law, as it relates to pollution, is working at its best when it has nothing to do – that is, when the deterrent effect is complete. The preventative power of an *ex post* liability system relies on the threat of action. Where rights are clearly defined, as with anglers and rivers, potential polluters know exactly what they can and cannot do. There is no doubt that the ACA's actions, based on common law protection of private rights over water and fishing, are a significant threat to would-be polluters. That few cases find their way to court merely shows the strength of the ACA's methods. An estimate of how much pollution it has prevented is impossible to calculate. Its more famous cases show that it has cleaned up (and kept clean) hundreds of miles of rivers in industrial areas, such as the Derwent, Trent and Dee (estuary).

The extremely successful and efficient out-of-court settlement of disputes means that the ACA is not well known to the general public. It is obvious from the *ACA Reviews* that it has always been a struggle for the ACA staff to maintain membership. When the ACA was bringing actions (and receiving newspaper coverage) its membership kept increasing, from 1,500 in 1950 to over 12,000 in 1966. As the powerful common law deterrent became widely known in local authority and business circles, any disputes were quickly settled in the anglers' favour. Even members who had directly benefited from ACA actions forgot to renew their subscriptions because the threat of pollution had been removed so effectually. Membership declined until the notable actions of the 1980s, and then rose to 16,500 in July 2000 (of which 2,000 are club members, representing over 250,000 anglers in total – see Figure 1).

The ACA rarely failed, but was particularly frustrated by polluters, especially local councils, which were given statutory authority to pollute. The breach of private rights in the name of public interest was a pervasive and insidious form of government intervention, but the ACA worked through the parliamentary process to challenge the authority. Despite pollution being made a criminal offence in 1876, it was not until Part II of the Control of Pollution Act (1974) came into effect in the mid-1980s that regulation really began to tackle pollution with any effect.

The era of government listening primarily to producer interests did not really end until 1989, with privatisation. From then on, consumer interest groups (if not consumers themselves) were those most dominant in establishing government policy. Over-zealous bureaucrats and interest groups could, in the future, hamper anglers as much as pollution did in the past, by preventing change to the river environment and undermining the value of fisheries.

Almost as remarkable as the ACA's legal action was its lobbying activity. Working within its specific brief to establish and maintain clean rivers, the ACA became a successful environmental watchdog long before the major environmental groups were formed. Had it not been for ACA lobbying, government Acts between 1951 and 1985 would have protected nationalised industries from all liability for pollution. It is extremely doubtful whether government, national or local, would have prevented gross pollution of English and Welsh rivers.

Figure 1 ACA members

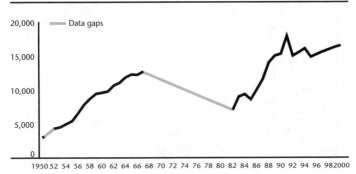

Membership of the ACA increased steadily well into the 1960s. Membership was reported sporadically for a while in the *ACA Reviews*, presumably as membership was falling. There were no high profile cases in this time. Membership starts to be recorded again regularly from the late 1980s. The peak recorded in 1991 is probably an overestimate (as lapsed members would have been removed at the end of the year). Membership has been around 15,000 in the past decade although it is now increasing. As well as individual members, there are about 2,000 club memberships, which means that ACA defends the fishing of over 250,000 anglers.

Modern environmental organisations have grown to resemble the large corporations that they attack. They rely on orchestrated publicity events to raise donations to support their massive administration. They lobby support from large donors and have all but forgotten the individual supporters on whom they were founded. The ACA, which has never had more than five employees, has thankfully been spared the temptation to abandon its basic interests. It occasionally reviews the latest scares (acid rain, pesticide residues, global warming) but it recognises that these topics are tangential to its main aim, and the review editors always treat the issues sensibly.

In the fifty years since the prescient John Eastwood founded the ACA, the various solicitors and barristers acting on behalf of its members have probably had over 2,000 cases of pollution referred to them. About 40 per cent of the cases involved local

Figure 2 **Reported injunctions in first 25 years**

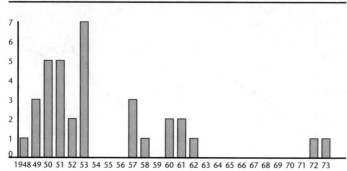

Following publicity surrounding ACA cases it became clear that the duty of care owed to riparian owners was usually greater than that required by legislation. Polluters soon realised the power of injunctions and were more willing to co-operate to remove a nuisance than to go to court to fight it out.

authorities or companies operating with statutory authority. Private companies were potential defendants in 47 per cent of the cases; about 7 per cent were farmers and there is a small miscellaneous remainder. A total of 920 cases has been collated so far by the author in an ever-expanding database, and many more will be added over the coming years.

In the author's database, there are 34 recorded injunctions (most before 1963 – see Figure 2) and damages and costs totalling considerably more than £1 million against defendants (a much greater amount in present-day prices). Once anglers' rights were established, few cases brought direct challenges. As the defendants' lawyers became aware of the strength of the ACA case, most disputes were settled out of court. The ACA reported that 'large, undisclosed settlements' were being achieved from the late 1960s onwards (ACA, 1974, 20: 1). There are probably far more injunctions, court orders and verbal agreements made than this author has been able to unearth. Furthermore, the total of settlements is probably nearer £10 million (at least £32 million) because settlements often remain undisclosed, since most defendants wish to keep their names out of the press. In its history, the ACA has lost only three court actions.

Most of the cases never reached the courts, and of those only a handful were ever reported in law reports/journals, a few of those mentioned above being the exceptions. Legal representatives for the ACA became adept at negotiating settlements by the threat of action.

> We have always taken the view that by far the greater part of existing pollution has not been caused deliberately, but through lack of forethought, ignorance, and a non-realization of the damage that can be done to fishing and the purity of our rivers. (*ACA Review* editorial, 1951)

Now a team of three lawyers (one working full time for the ACA) and an ACA staff of four (who also work on membership and other matters) are able to maintain forty cases a year as an average, a remarkable achievement of efficiency and simplicity.

The ACA campaigns against pollution, not against particular polluters. Nor does it try to rally public opinion to force changes through Parliament; it simply protects the civil rights that the common man has in his property. This thoroughly single-minded campaign against pollution has probably been the most successful that any nation has seen from a voluntary organisation.

There were over 1.1 million anglers registered in England and Wales in 1998 (and over 500,000 when the ACA was formed). This is a massive user base from which to draw support, and an ever-vigilant membership primed to spot pollution. It is unlikely that any other interest group would have as many potential members with a similar goal (although the Royal Society for the Protection of Birds claims a million members).

Part of the success of the ACA is that it relies on a system of law where the individual's rights are narrowly defined and can be strictly upheld. ACA actions are, on the whole, not general citizen suits against threats to the environment, but specific actions against individual polluters, brought by people with strong claims and legal standing. Any country with similar common rights could use the ACA methods as a template to exercise individual rights in the environment. (See Landry, 1998, for a discussion of the situation in the USA.)

What should the ACA do in the future?

When the ACA started out there was little public or governmental sympathy with its aims. Even now that we are all environmentalists, anglers' interests still do not coincide exactly with the mainstream view. Anglers want clean rivers because they support fish – other benefits are incidental – and it is this narrow definition of interests and protection of rights in those interests which gives the ACA its strength.

The ACA's success has come from its defence of civil rights, and in urging individuals and co-operatives (clubs) to acquire property rights in the environment in which they pursue their leisure interests. Political 'ownership' of the environment in the past has led to environmental degradation and pollution. There is now serious political interest in environmental protection, but a successful outcome is far from certain. Government has tried several times to override the common law interests with new policies designed to protect the environment, and each time those policies have been found ineffectual. By contrast, the system of protection of property rights in the civil courts has shown itself to be beneficial, efficient, flexible and equitable.

Several Acts of Parliament since 1963 have tried and failed to establish instream flow requirements for each river (Carty & Payne, 1998). Without levels being established, discharge and abstraction consents always run the risk of harming the environment. The result is that, even today, when environmental interests dominate in water legislation formulation, common law is still required to protect fish and the water in which they live. The common law says that it is the duty of the discharger to ensure that the receiving environment can dilute his effluent without causing pollution. This is a simple test which encompasses all circumstances and provides certainty for all water users.

If the government follows such ill-defined policies as the 'precautionary principle' and 'sustainable development', the results could easily be perverse. The example of the River Frome (see pp. 105–6) shows that fishery owners, who have the strongest interest in maintaining the quality of their waters, might have their powers removed by over-zealous officials. Sustainable development can be interpreted as no or little development, with the removal of industrial and even leisure activities from our waterways.

The ACA may be best advised to concentrate on maintaining individual rights and restricting the powers that the Environment Agency has over rivers. For example, the ACA could take advantage of the proposed changes in legislation to allow it to buy up abstraction licences (perhaps from farmers), to ensure that the water they need stays within the streams. Ownership of the environment is the best way to ensure that it is protected. In the same way that the ACA Guarantee Fund helped fight pollution, perhaps an in-stream flow fund could be established, to work to the model established by angling and environmental groups in the western United States (see Landry, 1998).

It is also worth mentioning that, compared with the larger and better-known groups which now take an interest in the environment, the ACA has a very small staff. Where it sticks to its main interests the ACA is highly efficient, but where its voice is simply echoing other groups its time and meagre resources are probably poorly spent. Perhaps the greatest challenge, and one the ACA has not yet taken up, will be to fight for individual rights in the face of extremist pressure from socialists masquerading as environmentalists.

APPENDIX   ACA MEMBERSHIP AND VALUE OF FEES

There is no doubt that the ACA has reduced the loss of fisheries throughout UK waters. While it is impossible to be exact, it is likely that fisheries declined in quality and number in the second quarter of the twentieth century. Since the 1980s, both the quality and quantity of fisheries have improved markedly (NRA, 1994). In nominal terms, the ACA subscription fee has increased ten times, from £1 to £10. Over the same period the aggregate increase in price in a sample (taken by the author) of mixed fisheries is over fifty times (salmon and trout fisheries have increased in price by more than coarse fisheries). In that respect membership of the ACA is over five times better value than it was fifty years ago (see Figure 3a).

In real terms (adjusting for retail price increases) the ACA fee is about half what it was in 1948 (in other words, to match inflation the ACA membership fee should be approximately £20 instead of £10), whereas the real value of fisheries is over 2.5 times what it was in 1948. For most game fisheries it is over three times greater (see Figure 3b). According to Williamson (1991: 18), the capital value of some salmon fisheries can be as much as £15,000 per fish caught per average year.

Given that ACA action and general awareness have increased the available supply of fisheries in England and Wales, the price of fisheries should fall, all else being equal. Therefore, since prices

Figure 3a **Comparison of ACA fee and fishery values**
Fishery value data based on £1 in 1948

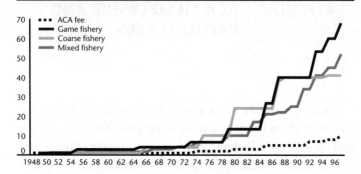

Source: Where to Fish, 64th–85th editions, and original sources.

Figure 3b **Inflation-adjusted ACA fee and fishery values**
Fishery value data based on £1 in 1948

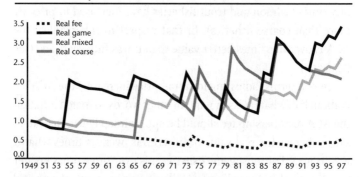

All data are in 1998 prices, adjusted by the retail price index.

have risen 2.5 times above inflation, at a time of increasing supply of fisheries, demand must have increased significantly.

ACA actions in urban areas have helped to preserve fisheries near to where most people live. According to the National Angling Survey of 1980, people join clubs to have 'access to good and/or local waters'. Easy access to local fisheries is also likely to have encouraged young people to take up angling. A survey by the Angling Foundation showed a 3 per cent increase in the number of anglers between 1986 and 1989, bringing the total to nearly 4 million, nearly half of whom were under 25 years old. Coarse fishing represented 58 per cent of the total and game fishing 23 per cent.

It is likely that the value of fisheries will have been underestimated in the past since much of the value was absorbed in non-direct fishing costs, such as travelling longer distances to find fishing. The creation or restoration of more fishing water has relieved congestion on unpolluted water, although the value of this is very difficult to measure.

REFERENCES

ACA Reviews, 1948–2000.

Anderson, T. L. (1984), *Water Rights: Scarce Resource Allocation, Bureaucracy, and the Environment*, Ballinger, Cambridge, Massachusetts.

Anderson, T. L., and D. Leal (1991), *Free Market Environmentalism*, Pacific Research Institute, San Francisco, California.

Anderson, T. L., and P. Hill (1975), 'The Evolution of Property Rights: A Study of the American West', *Journal of Law and Economics*, 12: 163.

Bate, R. N. (1993), 'Coase's Lighthouse', *Economic Affairs*, 13: 4.

——— (1994), *English and Welsh Rivers: A Common Law Approach to Pollution Prevention*, Master's thesis, Cambridge University.

——— (2000), 'Protecting English and Welsh Rivers: The Role of the Anglers Conservation Association', *The Common Law and the Environment*, ed. R. Meiners and A. Morriss, Rowman and Littlefield, Oxford.

Benson, B. (1990), *The Enterprise of Law*, Pacific Research Institute, San Francisco, California.

Birmingham Post (1952), John Eastwood obituary, 2 February.

Blackstone, W. (1765–9), *Commentaries of the Laws of England*.

Brenner, J. (1974), 'Nuisance Law and the Industrial Revolution' *Journal of Legal Studies*, 3: 403.

Buchanan, J., and G. Tullock (1962), *The Calculus of Consent*,

University of Michigan Press, Ann Arbor, Michigan.

Calabresi, G., and D. Melamed (1972), 'Property Rules, Liability Rules and Inalienability: One View of the Cathedral', *Harvard Law Review*, 85: 1089.

Carty, P. (2000), personal communication, 10 November.

Carty, P., and S. Payne (1998), *Angling and the Law*, Merlin Unwin, Shropshire.

Coase, R. (1974), 'The Lighthouse in Economics', *Journal of Law and Economics*, 17 (2): 357–76.

Cooter, R., and T. Ulen (1988), *Law and Economics*, HarperCollins, London.

Eastwood, H. (2000), personal communication, 6 July.

Gerrish. C. S. (1973), *Pollution: The ACA Handbook*, ACA, Bury St Edmunds.

Green, D. (1994), *Reinventing Civil Society*, Institute of Economic Affairs, London.

Hodges, D. (2000), personal communication, 5 July.

Juergensmeyer, J. (1972), 'Common Law Remedies and Protection of the Environment', *University of British Columbia Law Review*, 6: 215–36.

Kolstad, C. D., T. S. Ulen and G. V. Johnson (1990), 'Ex-post liability for harm vs. Ex-ante Safety Regulation: Substitutes or Complements?', *American Economic Review*, 80 (4).

Krier, J. (1992), 'The Tragedy of the Commons, Part Two', *Harvard Journal of Law and Public Policy*, 15 (2).

Landry, C. (1998), *Saving Our Streams*, PERC discussion paper, Bozeman, Montana.

Maxey, M. (1999), *Nuclear Energy; Environmental Problem or Solution?*, European Science and Environment Forum. Cambridge.

Meiners, R. E., and B. Yandle (1992), 'Constitutional Choice for the Control of Water Pollution', *Constitutional Political Economy*, 3 (3): 359–80.

—— (eds) (1993), *The Economic Consequences of Liability Rules: In Defense of Common Law Liability*, Quorum Books, New York, Connecticut, London.

Morris, J. (ed.) (2000), *Rethinking Risk: The Precautionary Principle Revisited*, Butterworth Heinemann, Oxford.

NRA (1994), *Water Quality in England and Wales*, National Rivers Authority, Peterborough.

Ogus, A. I. (1989), 'Law and Spontaneous Order: Hayek's Contribution to Legal Theory', *Journal of Law and Society*, 16 (4), winter: 393–409.

Ogus, A. I., and G. M. Richardson (1977), 'Economics and the Environment: A study of private nuisance', *Cambridge Law Journal*, 36 (2), November: 284–325.

Olson, M. (1965), *The Logic of Collective Action*, Harvard University Press, Cambridge, Massachusetts.

Ostrom, E. (1990), *Governing the Commons: the evolution of institutions for collective action*, Cambridge University Press, Cambridge.

Pennington, M. (1997), *Saving the Countryside: By Quango or Market*, Institute of Economic Affairs, London.

Rabkin, J., and J. Sheehan (1999), *Global Greens, Global Governance*, Institute of Economic Affairs, London

Radford, A. F. (1984), *The Economics and Value of Recreational Salmon Fisheries in England and Wales: An Analysis of the Rivers Wye, Mandach, Tamar and Lune*, CEMARE report No. 8.

Slocock, R. (2000), personal communication with Chairman of Piddle and Frome Fisheries Association, June.

Smith, K., and D. J. Keenan (1979), *English Law*, Pitman Publishing, London.

Solbe, J. (1988), *Water Quality for Salmon and Trout*, The Atlantic Salmon Trust, Perth.

Tromans, S. (1982), 'Nuisance – Prevention or Payment?', *Cambridge Law Journal*, 41 (1), April: 87–109.

Tullock, G. (1976), *The Vote Motive*, Institute of Economic Affairs, London.

Walton, Isaak (1653), *The Compleat Angler*.

Williamson, R. (1991a), *Salmon Fisheries in Scotland*, Atlantic Salmon Trust, Perth.

——— (1991b), 'Scottish salmon fishing rights, a transferable property: the consequences for administration and regulation', presented at ICREI Colloquium, Paris.

Wisdom. A. S. (1979), *The Law of Rivers and Watercourses*, Shaw & Sons Ltd, London.

CASES CITED

An asterisk indicates cases only reported in the ACA's records.

ACA Trustees Ltd v. British Coal (1992)*

ACA Trustees Ltd v. Northumbrian Water Authority (1983)*

ACA Trustees Ltd v. Thames Water Authority (1987)*

Bone v. Searle (1975) 1 All ER 787

Chasemore v. Richards (1859), 7 H.L. Cas. 349

Crossley v. Lightowler (1867), 16 L.T. 438

Golden Hill Fishing Club v. Wansford Trout Farm (1986)*

Leek and District Fly Fishing Club (Staffs branch) v. Severn Trent Water (1992)*

Lord Brocket v. Luton Corporation (1946)*

Myddelton and Others v. J. Summers and Sons Ltd (1954)*

Orpington and District Angling Association v. Vegetable Parchment Mills Ltd (1949)*

Pride of Derby and Derbyshire Angling Association Ltd and Earl of Harrington v. British Celanese Ltd, the Derby Corporation, the British Electrical Authority and Midland Tar Distillers (1952), 1 All ER 179; Court of Appeal, 1953, 1 All ER 1326

Sturges v. Bridgman (1879), 11 Ch. D. 852, 865

Upton v. Great Torrington Corporation (1951)*

Upton v. Torridge Vale Dairies (Devon) Limited (1951)*

William Aldred's Case (1611), 77 E.R. 816 K.B., cited in Juergensmeyer, 1972: 216

ABOUT THE IEA

The Institute is a research and educational charity (No. CC 235 351), limited by guarantee. Its mission is to improve understanding of the fundamental institutions of a free society with particular reference to the role of markets in solving economic and social problems.

The IEA achieves its mission by:

- a high quality publishing programme
- conferences, seminars, lectures and other events
- outreach to school and college students
- brokering media introductions and appearances

The IEA, which was established in 1955 by the late Sir Antony Fisher, is an educational charity, not a political organisation. It is independent of any political party or group and does not carry on activities intended to affect support for any political party or candidate in any election or referendum, or at any other time. It is financed by sales of publications, conference fees and voluntary donations.

In addition to its main series of publications the IEA also publishes a quarterly journal, *Economic Affairs*, and has two specialist programmes – Environment and Technology, and Education.

The IEA is aided in its work by a distinguished international Academic Advisory Council and an eminent panel of Honorary Fellows. Together with other academics, they review prospective IEA publications, their comments being passed on anonymously to authors. All IEA papers are therefore subject to the same rigorous independent refereeing process as used by leading academic journals.

IEA publications enjoy widespread classroom use and course adoptions in schools and universities. They are also sold throughout the world and often translated/reprinted.

Since 1974 the IEA has helped to create a world-wide network of 100 similar institutions in over 70 countries. They are all independent but share the IEA's mission.

Views expressed in the IEA's publications are those of the authors, not those of the Institute (which has no corporate view), its Managing Trustees, Academic Advisory Council members or senior staff.

Members of the Institute's Academic Advisory Council, Honorary Fellows, Trustees and Staff are listed on the following page.

The Institute gratefully acknowledges financial support for its publications programme and other work from a generous benefaction by the late Alec and Beryl Warren.

ie a

The Institute of Economic Affairs
2 Lord North Street, Westminster, London SW1P 3LB
Tel: 020 7799 8900
Fax: 020 7799 2137
Email: iea@iea.org.uk
Internet: iea.org.uk

General Director	John Blundell

Editorial Director	Professor Colin Robinson

Managing Trustees

Chairman: Professor D R Myddelton

Robert Boyd
Michael Fisher
Malcolm McAlpine
Sir Michael Richardson
Professor Martin Ricketts

Lord Vinson, LVO
Sir Peter Walters
Linda Whetstone
Professor Geoffrey E Wood

Academic Advisory Council

Chairman: Professor Martin Ricketts

Graham Bannock
Professor Norman Barry
Professor Michael Beenstock
Professor Donald J Boudreaux
Professor John Burton
Professor Forrest Capie
Professor Steven N S Cheung
Professor Tim Congdon
Professor N F R Crafts
Professor David de Meza
Professor Richard A Epstein
Nigel Essex
John Flemming
Professor David Greenaway
Walter E Grinder
Professor Steve H Hanke
Professor Keith Hartley
Dr R M Hartwell
Professor Peter M Jackson
Dr Jerry Jordan
Professor Daniel B Klein

Dr Anja Kluever
Professor David Laidler
Professor Stephen C Littlechild
Professor Antonio Martino
Dr Ingrid A Merikoski
Professor Patrick Minford
Professor David Parker
Professor Victoria Curzon Price
Professor Charles K Rowley
Professor Pascal Salin
Professor Pedro Schwartz
Professor J R Shackleton
Jane S Shaw
Professor W Stanley Siebert
Professor David Simpson
Professor Vernon L Smith
Professor Nicola Tynan
Professor Roland Vaubel
Professor E G West
Professor Lawrence H White
Professor Walter E Williams

Honorary Fellows

Professor Armen A Alchian
Sir Samuel Brittan
Professor James M Buchanan
Professor Ronald H Coase
Professor Terence W Hutchison
Professor Dennis S Lees
Professor Chiaki Nishiyama

Professor Sir Alan Peacock
Professor Ivor Pearce
Professor Ben Roberts
Professor Anna J Schwartz
Professor Gordon Tullock
Professor Sir Alan Walters
Professor Basil S Yamey

125

For information about subscriptions to IEA publications, please contact:

Subscriptions
The Institute of Economic Affairs
2 Lord North Street
London SW1P 3LB

Tel: 020 7799 8900
Fax: 020 7799 2137
Website: www.iea.org.uk/books/subscribe.htm

Other papers recently published by the IEA include:

WHO, What and Why?

Transnational Government, Legitimacy and the World Health Organization
Roger Scruton
Occasional Paper 113
ISBN 0 255 36487 3

The World Turned Rightside Up

A New Trading Agenda for the Age of Globalisation
John C. Hulsman
Occasional Paper 114
ISBN 0 255 36495 4

The Representation of Business in English Literature

Introduced and edited by Arthur Pollard
Readings 53
ISBN 0 255 36491 1

Anti-Liberalism 2000

The Rise of New Millennium Collectivism
David Henderson
Occasional Paper 115
ISBN 0 255 36497 0

Capitalism, Morality and Markets

Brian Griffiths, Robert A. Sirico, Norman Barry and Frank Field
Readings 54
ISBN 0 255 36496 2

A Conversation with Harris and Seldon

Ralph Harris and Arthur Seldon
Occasional Paper 116
ISBN 0 255 36498 9

Malaria and the DDT Story

Richard Tren & Roger Bate
Occasional Paper 117
ISBN 0 255 36499 7

A Plea to Economists Who Favour Liberty: Assist the Everyman

Daniel B. Klein
Occasional Paper 118
ISBN 0 255 36501 2

Waging the War of Ideas

John Blundell
Occasional Paper 119
ISBN 0 255 36500 4

To order copies of currently available IEA papers, or to enquire about availability, please contact:

Lavis Marketing
73 Lime Walk
Oxford OX3 7AD

Tel: 01865 767575
Fax: 01865 750079
Email: orders@lavismarketing.co.uk